Praise for *The Teach*

CU01033973

The Teacher's Guide to SEN is both pı
read for teachers, SENCOs and schoo ......understand
how best to support the needs of all learners. Highly recommended!

Professor Dame Alison Peacock, CEO, Chartered College of Teaching

The Teacher's Guide to SEN demystifies the jargon and complex issues
surrounding students' additional needs. Filled with helpful, practical,
classroom-based strategies and case studies it reassures and guides in
equal measure. Apply these techniques so you can make 'reasonable
adjustments' and provide high-quality learning experiences for all your
students, irrespective of their individual starting points.

Carmel Bones, education consultant, AST, trainer and author

Natalie Packer uses her expertise, knowledge and vast experience in SEN
to produce a book that should be read by every new teacher entering the
profession. *The Teacher's Guide to SEN* balances theoretical approaches
to supporting children with special educational needs with helpful ideas
and case studies that are rooted in current practice. It is a book that offers
the reader the opportunity to critically reflect on their own practice and
empowers teachers to put in place practical strategies that will genuinely
make a difference to learning in the classroom.

David Bartram OBE, Director of SEND, London Leadership Strategy

A fantastic, practical resource. This book demystifies the world of SEN
so that every teacher can exhibit inclusive practice to meet the needs of a
wide range of learners. The combination of brief case studies, key ideas
from research, links to further resources and instant things to try makes
this book a unique CPD tool for busy teachers.

Maria Constantinou, Deputy Head and Inclusion Leader,
St Mary's C of E Primary School

In *The Teacher's Guide to SEN* (her follow-up to *The Perfect SENCO*) Natalie Packer demystifies SEN. The first part of the book gives an overview of SEN and what it means to be an inclusive teacher in practice. In the second part, each of the four main areas of SEN is covered in turn, in a very clear and user-friendly way. Finding useful tips and strategies is made easy with the use of icons throughout. This is a really practical and readable guide. This book will contribute to an increased knowledge and understanding of SEN at a critical time in the implementation of the government's reforms.

Malcolm Reeve, Executive Director for SEND and Inclusion,
Academies Enterprise Trust, National Leader of Education,
National College for Teaching and Leadership

Natalie draws on her wealth of experience and knowledge of SEN, plus the best available evidence, to produce this essential trove of key information and reflective and practical activities. The actionable strategies to support learners across the common areas of need are built on core components of high-quality teaching that work for all. This book demystifies the process of removing barriers to learning and will help new and practising teachers alike to develop confident and independent learners.

Rob Webster, Researcher, Centre for Inclusive Education,
UCL Institute of Education

Natalie Packer

The
Teacher's
GUIDE to
SEN

Crown House Publishing Limited
www.crownhouse.co.uk

First published by

Crown House Publishing Ltd
Crown Buildings, Bancyfelin, Carmarthen, Wales, SA33 5ND, UK
www.crownhouse.co.uk

and

Crown House Publishing Company LLC
PO Box 2223, Williston, VT 05495
www.crownhousepublishing.com

First published 2017

Cover photograph © kolidzei – fotolia.com

Case studies and additional ideas have been reproduced with the kind permission of
Hannah Ogden, Sarah March, Heather Fyfe, Alex Aldridge, Bruce Waelend, Cate
Marsden, Shenaz Ibrahim, Ruth Newbury, Andrew Crossley, Amjad Ali, Maria
Constantinou, Mandy Nicholls, Matt Smith and Laura Senn.

British Library Cataloguing-in-Publication Data
A catalogue entry for this book is available from the British Library.

Print ISBN 978-178583025-9
Mobi ISBN 978-178583218-5
ePub ISBN 978-178583219-2
ePDF ISBN 978-178583220-8

LCCN 2015953350

Printed and bound in the UK by
Gomer Press, Llandysul, Ceredigion

I dedicate this book to my beautiful niece Lexi, who was born part way through the writing process and whose existence constantly reminds me of the pure joy a child brings into our lives.

Acknowledgements

Thank you to all the amazing teachers and SENCOs who have provided me with ideas and case studies for this book. Thank you also to my husband Frank for his encouragement and patience, and to my 'unofficial editor' Helen for trying to keep me on track throughout this rather long journey!

Contents

Introduction

When you think about the pupils you teach, which ones immediately spring to mind? Is it the pupils who seem to effortlessly complete learning tasks and make progress easily? Is it the pupils who sit quietly in the corner of the classroom and just 'get on with things'? Or is it the pupils who find school difficult, display challenging behaviour and appear to require constant support to stay on task? It's probably the latter! The amount of time and energy focused on certain individuals as a result of their personalised learning needs can appear to be disproportionately high. However, every child has the right to be given the opportunity to succeed at school. For some, additional and targeted investment in them is exactly what they need in order to achieve.

The profile of pupils we teach today is very different to that of twenty (or even ten) years ago. Advancements in medicine have led to an increase in neonatal survival rates, meaning there are more pupils in our schools with complex learning difficulties and disabilities. A greater number of children and young people are now identified as having mental health problems, perhaps caused by traumatic early childhood experiences or external pressures, such as exam stress or the negative impact of social media. As professionals, we also have a greater awareness of the range of challenges children are experiencing and understand that their needs may be as a result of a variety of cognitive, communication, physical or emotional factors.

September 2014 brought with it some of the most significant changes to the national system for special educational needs (SEN) that we have seen for a long time. The introduction of the new Special Educational Needs and Disability Code of Practice raised the bar in terms of what is expected of teachers.[1] One of the key messages of the code is that *every* teacher is responsible and accountable for *every* pupil in their class,

1   Department for Education, *Special Educational Needs and Disability Code of Practice: 0 to 25 Years* (2014). Ref: DFE-00205-2013. Available at: https://www.gov.uk/government/publications/send-code-of-practice-0-to-25.

including those with SEN. So what does this mean in practice for you as a class or subject teacher? Essentially, it requires you to understand every individual's needs, have a range of knowledge and skills you can apply in the classroom and have the confidence to try out some new approaches. This isn't always easy, particularly when you may feel under pressure to demonstrate progress and achieve constantly improving results. However, being an inclusive teacher and getting great outcomes go hand in hand: what's good practice for pupils with SEN is, more often than not, good practice for all.

The information and advice given within this book is based on the assumption that, with a positive attitude, quality support and high aspirations, everyone can learn (albeit every child's learning priorities may be different). Your role is to enable all pupils to learn as effectively as possible. As committed teachers, we strive to do the best we can for all the children and young people we teach. If a pupil has SEN, this can often bring additional challenges for us as professionals, and this is where some guidance and support can be helpful.

The Teacher's Guide to SEN is for all primary and secondary teachers. It will be useful to those still training, those in the early stages of their careers and those more experienced practitioners who would like to refresh their knowledge or gather some new ideas to try in the classroom. Although the book has been predominantly written with teachers in mind, it will also be helpful to other education professionals who work with children and young people with SEN, including teaching assistants (TAs). The main aims of the book are:

- To give you an overview of SEN.

- To consolidate your understanding of what constitutes inclusive, high-quality teaching (HQT) for all pupils.

- To develop your knowledge of the main areas of SEN.

- To suggest strategies and ideas to use when teaching pupils with particular needs.

- To provide an opportunity for you to reflect on your own practice in relation to SEN.

The book is divided into two parts:

Part 1: The inclusive teacher

This part has been written to give you an overall insight into what is meant by SEN. It aims to clarify your key responsibilities in providing HQT for all pupils and SEN support for some, where required. It also highlights the importance of working in partnership to meet the needs of those with SEN, for example with parents and TAs.

Part 2: The teacher's toolkit

This part focuses on the broad areas of need, as outlined in the Special Educational Needs and Disability Code of Practice. It provides guidance on potential barriers to learning and offers practical strategies for supporting pupils with specific needs, such as moderate learning difficulties, autism and dyslexia. It does not aim to provide a comprehensive guide on every single learning need (now that would be a large publication!) but rather focuses on some of the most common areas of need you are likely to come across. There are examples of further resources which can be used to support each area of need covered. Part 2 has been written to dip in and out of, so you can visit the chapters most relevant to your needs or interests.

In each chapter you will find a wealth of information, underpinned by theory and research, and practical, hands-on ideas that can be used in the primary and/or secondary classroom. Each chapter contains the following:

 Did you know?

Interesting facts and examples from research which will help build your knowledge of SEN and address some common misconceptions.

Try it!

Practical activities for you to try in your classroom.

 Case studies

Examples of great practice from a range of teachers and other professionals involved in supporting children and young people with SEN.

 Reflect

Questions to ask yourself, to reflect on how you currently teach and consider how you could put some of the ideas into practice in your classroom (so you can have an even greater impact on learning!).

 Further resources

Examples of publications or websites that provide additional information on the topics covered in the chapter.

Although this book lists common barriers to learning and examples of strategies for pupils with different needs, this is not to suggest that if we simply apply the list of ideas, we will have all the solutions. Children with SEN are far too complex for that! No two children with SEN are the same and so no one way of teaching will be suitable for every child, even if they have similar areas of need.

Ultimately, this book is about teaching and learning for *all* pupils, including those with SEN. As committed teachers, we strive to do the best we can for all our pupils. We must recognise that some pupils will take longer to learn than others or will learn in different ways. Therefore we will need to be flexible and adapt our teaching to suit them. That's what makes teaching inclusive.

Part 1

The inclusive teacher

Chapter 1

What are special educational needs?

Defining SEN

Imagine it's the start of the year and you've been given a new class list by a member of the senior leadership team (SLT) or your head of department. They tell you that this is a class with 'lots of SEN'. (Clearly they think you're up to the challenge!) What are your initial thoughts? What information will you need about the pupils? And what does 'having SEN' actually mean anyway?

The term special educational needs is one that has been used within education for a number of years. It refers to children and young people who have learning difficulties or disabilities that make it significantly harder for them to learn or access education than most of their peers. A formal definition of SEN is given on page 15 of the Special Educational Needs and Disability Code of Practice:

> A child or young person has SEN if they have a learning difficulty or disability which calls for special educational provision to be made for him or her.

According to the code, a pupil has a learning difficulty if they have:

- a significantly greater difficulty in learning than the majority of their peers of the same age, or

- a disability that prevents or hinders them from making use of the facilities generally provided for their peers (this includes difficulties in accessing the curriculum)

Learning difficulties and disabilities cover a wide range of issues, including challenges in acquiring basic skills, specific difficulties with reading, writing, numeracy or motor skills, communication problems, emotional difficulties, mental health issues, sensory needs, physical needs, etc. This is by no means an exhaustive list and later on in this chapter you will come across further information about the broad areas of need which are identified within the Code of Practice. Whatever the difficulty might be, however, the pupil will require special educational provision to help remove potential barriers to learning.

Special educational provision

If delivering high-quality lessons is the norm for you, no doubt you'll be meeting the needs of most of the pupils in your class. But even as a brilliant teacher, you will still come across some pupils who require *additional* provision. Additional provision goes beyond the differentiated approaches and learning arrangements that we would usually expect to be in place as part of HQT. Special educational provision *may* include some, or all, of the following:

- A highly personalised curriculum and individual timetable – e.g. a curriculum that includes life skills lessons.

- Specialist resources or equipment – e.g. a wheelchair, communication aids.

- The use of specific and individualised strategies in the classroom – e.g. time out, alternative forms of communication.

- Additional interventions to target basic skills – e.g. literacy or numeracy group intervention.

- Additional support from an adult or peer – e.g. support from a TA.

- Support with physical or personal care difficulties – e.g. eating, toileting, getting around school safely.

- Input from other professionals – e.g. specialist teachers, educational psychologists, speech and language therapists.

- Individualised learning plans that identify specific targets and outline the special educational provision to be put in place.

Schools have a duty to make special educational provision available for any pupil who needs it. This means that every teacher within the school has a responsibility to deliver HQT and to support any special educational provision in place for individuals.

 Did you know?

Just over 14 per cent of pupils in the UK are currently identified as having SEN.[1] On average, that equates to approximately four pupils in every mainstream class.

A little bit of history

In the UK today, there is no question over the right of pupils with SEN to be included within our education system. However, this was not always the case. When compulsory schooling began in the late 1800s, many children with learning disabilities were deemed to be 'uneducable' and so were denied the formal right to any education. Some provision existed for deaf, blind, 'defective' and epileptic children under the Elementary Education (Blind and Deaf Children) Act 1893 and the Elementary Education (Defective and Epileptic Children) Act 1899. However, it was almost one hundred years later before any significant change took place when the Education (Handicapped Children) Act 1970 was introduced to ensure entitlement to an education for every child, irrespective of their needs or difficulties.[2]

In the late 1970s the government set up an inquiry, led by the Warnock Committee, to look at the needs of children who required additional provision in school. The committee's report[3] gave rise to the Education

---

1   Department for Education, *Special Educational Needs in England: January 2016* (2016). Ref: SFR 29/2016. Available at: https://www.gov.uk/government/uploads/system/uploads/attachment_data/file/539158/SFR29_2016_Main_Text.pdf.

2   See http://www.legislation.gov.uk/ukpga/1970/52/enacted.

3   HMSO, *Report of the Committee of Enquiry into the Education of Handicapped Children and Young People* (1978). Available at: http://www.educationengland.org.uk/documents/warnock/warnock1978.html.

Act 1981, introducing the term 'special educational needs' and establishing statements of need, which were legal documents outlining provision for pupils at the most severe end of the SEN continuum.[4]

A series of other acts, legislation and statutory guidance have since followed, all of which have aimed to increasingly promote the inclusion of pupils with SEN in the education system. This included the Special Educational Needs and Disability Act 2001,[5] which prevented discrimination against people with disabilities in their access to education, and the Special Educational Needs Code of Practice 2001.[6] The code, which provided a clear framework for identifying, assessing and meeting the needs of pupils with SEN, was based on the general principles introduced by the SEN and Disability Act. These included the right for a child with SEN to have their needs met (normally within a mainstream school), to have their views and those of their parents considered and to have access to a broad, balanced and relevant curriculum.

By 2011, the SEN system that had been in place for ten years was no longer fit for purpose so a new legislative act and Special Educational Needs and Disability Code of Practice were consulted on and finally introduced in 2014. The Children and Families Act extends the previous system for SEN so that it covers children and young people with SEN from birth, right up to the age of 25.[7] The Act gives children, young people and their parents greater control and choice in ensuring needs are properly met. The Act also replaces the previous statements of SEN with education, health and care (EHC) plans. The EHC plan describes all the child's needs and long-term outcomes, in addition to detailing the specialist help and provision required to meet them.

---

4   Education Act (1981). Available at: http://www.educationengland.org.uk/documents/acts/1981-education-act.pdf.
5   See http://www.legislation.gov.uk/ukpga/2001/10/contents.
6   Department for Education, *Special Educational Needs Code of Practice* (2001). Ref: DfES/581/2001. Available at: http://webarchive.nationalarchives.gov.uk/20130401151715/https://www.education.gov.uk/publications/eorderingdownload/dfes%200581%20200mig2228.pdf.
7   See http://www.legislation.gov.uk/ukpga/2014/6/contents/enacted.

Try it!

Read all about it!

Maintained schools and academies must publish a SEN Information Report on their website giving information to parents about the SEN provision in the school. Have a look at your school's SEN Information Report on their website (and also the SEN policy) as this should provide a good overview of the provision your school has in place for pupils with SEN.

The Special Educational Needs and Disability Code of Practice: 0 to 25 years

The Special Educational Needs and Disability Code of Practice provides guidance and advice to schools (as well as local authorities (LAs) and other organisations) about how to identify, assess and make provision for children and young people with SEN. The code outlines the actions that schools should take to meet the needs of pupils with SEN by removing barriers to learning and putting high-quality provision in place. It also includes information on how education, health and social care providers should be working together to meet the needs of children and young people with SEN and how EHC plans work.

The guidance in the Code of Practice is designed to encourage the following:

- Early identification of SEN and early intervention to support a child or young person once their needs have been identified.

- Greater choice and control for children, young people and parents over the support to be provided (the views, wishes and feelings of those directly involved must always be considered).

- Collaboration between education, health and social care services to provide a range of support for young people with SEN.

- High-quality provision in schools and other settings to meet the needs of children and young people with SEN.

- Support to enable young people with SEN to become increasingly independent as they move from childhood into young adulthood.

As a professional working alongside pupils with SEN, it is important you are able to apply these principles where appropriate: for example, by contributing to the identification of a pupil's needs or by providing HQT and support.

Areas of SEN

The Code of Practice identifies four broad areas of need and support. The four areas can be used by schools to review and manage their special educational provision, as they give an overview of the range of needs that should be planned for. Although the purpose of the broad areas is not to 'label' children or try to fit them into a box, you may find the categories useful for thinking about some of the general areas of special needs that you will need to plan for within your own class:

1. **Communication and interaction**

    This category includes speech, language and communication needs (SLCN), for example, difficulty in using language and/or understanding language. It also includes conditions where there are challenges with understanding social rules of communication, for example autistic spectrum disorder (ASD).

2. **Cognition and learning**

    This category covers a wide range of needs where pupils learn at a slower pace than others their age. Pupils may have difficulty in understanding parts of the curriculum or have difficulties with organisation and memory skills. It includes moderate learning difficulties (MLD), severe learning difficulties (SLD) and pro-found and multiple learning difficulties (PMLD). It also includes specific learning difficulties (SpLD), such as dyslexia, dyspraxia and dyscalculia.

3. **Social, emotional and mental health difficulties**

   This category includes difficulties that can manifest as withdrawn, isolated, challenging or disturbing behaviour, or difficulties that mean pupils face challenges in managing their relationships with others. Examples include mental health difficulties such as anxiety or depression, self-harming, substance misuse and eating disorders. Social, emotional and mental health (SEMH) difficulties also include attention deficit disorder (ADD), attention deficit hyperactivity disorder (ADHD) and attachment disorder (AD).

4. **Sensory and/or physical needs**

   This category includes visual impairment (VI), hearing impairment (HI) and multi-sensory impairment (MSI). It also includes physical disabilities (PD) that require additional ongoing support and/or specialist equipment.

 Did you know?

The most common area of need reported for pupils with SEN in mainstream schools is MLD. Over a quarter of pupils identified with SEN in 2016 were recorded as having this type of need.[8] It is possible, however, that some of these pupils may have an undiagnosed SpLD or speech and language need.

In reality, an individual child or young person will often have needs that cut across two or more of the areas. In addition to social communication difficulties, a pupil with ASD, for example, may also have cognitive

---

8 Department for Education, *Schools, Pupils and Their Characteristics: January 2016* (2016). Ref: SFR 20/2016. Available at: https://www.gov.uk/government/statistics/schools-pupils-and-their-characteristics-january-2016, p. 14.

difficulties, social issues and/or sensory impairment. Similarly, the individual profile of one pupil identified with a particular need is likely to be very different to the profile of another pupil identified under the same category. It is therefore important to understand the *individual* needs of any child in order to be able to meet their needs effectively, rather than focusing on the 'label'. Part 2 provides further information on some of the areas of need mentioned previously.

SEN and disability

The definition outlined earlier in this chapter refers to pupils with SEN. However, you may have noticed that the document providing the definition is called the Special Educational Needs *and Disability* Code of Practice. There is a separate definition of disability which is outlined in the Equality Act 2010.[9] This Act states that schools cannot unlawfully discriminate against pupils because of their disability (or other 'protected characteristics' including race, religion and sexual orientation). The Equality Act states that a person has a disability if they have a physical or mental impairment and that impairment has a substantial and long-term adverse effect on their ability to carry out normal day-to-day activities.

This definition includes learning difficulties, language and communication impairments, mental health conditions and medical conditions (normal day-to-day activities cover sleeping, eating, walking, talking, learning and so on ...). Therefore, many pupils who have SEN (including those with significant dyslexia or autism) will also be defined as being disabled under the Equality Act. Not all pupils who are defined as disabled will have SEN though. For children with diabetes, severe asthma or arthritis, for example, special educational provision may *not* necessarily be required to meet their needs.

Under the Equality Act, discrimination includes treating a pupil with a disability less favourably because they are disabled, or putting them at a substantial disadvantage compared with another child who is not

---

9   Department for Education, *Equality Act 2010 and Schools: Departmental Advice for School Leaders, School Staff, Governing Bodies and Local Authorities* (2014). Ref: DFE-00296-2013. Available at: http://www.gov.uk/government/uploads/system/uploads/attachment_data/file/315587/Equality_Act_Advice_Final.pdf.

disabled. Every school, and every member of staff within that school, has a duty to ensure that discrimination does not occur. This is called the 'reasonable adjustments duty' and it means schools must be proactive in making 'reasonable adjustments' for pupils with SEN and disabilities, to prevent discrimination.

So, what does making 'reasonable adjustments' mean for you as a teacher? In practice, you are already likely to be implementing reasonable adjustments in your classroom. An adjustment might involve changing the way you set up your classroom so pupils with limited mobility can access it more easily, or being aware of the level of language you use with pupils who have communication difficulties, or introducing buddy schemes to provide peer support. The list on page 18 gives further examples of reasonable adjustments.

 Try it!

Accessing reading material

If pupils are using texts, worksheets or other reading material in the lesson, make sure they are pitched at a suitable level. For a quick way to check if the readability level of a text is suitable for a younger pupil, encourage them to use the five-finger rule. Give them the text and ask them to read the first page or passage. Each time they cannot read a word, they raise a finger. If five fingers are raised by the time they reach the end of the page or passage, this means the text is likely to be too difficult for them to read comfortably.

For older pupils, the online SMOG (Simplified Measure of Gobbledygook!) test provides a measure of readability by calculating the reading-age level of a piece of text. Simply copy and paste the text you want to measure into the online calculator and the SMOG readability score will be calculated: http://www.niace.org.uk/misc/SMOG-calculator/smogcalc.php.

Making reasonable adjustments in my classroom

- My classroom layout provides access for pupils with limited mobility – e.g. space for wheelchair users to move around, appropriate table height. ☐

- I display classroom signs in a range of media – e.g. Braille, symbols. ☐

- I ensure all areas of the classroom are appropriately illuminated to support pupils with VI. ☐

- My classroom has appropriate acoustics to support pupils with HI. ☐

- There is a distraction-free learning area for pupils with ASD to use if needed. ☐

- I consider the language I use to model, explain and give instructions. I check that pupils with communication difficulties understand these instructions. ☐

- Any written materials I provide can be accessed by pupils with reading difficulties – e.g. they are at an appropriate reading level, the format and content are clear. ☐

- I provide extra time to enable pupils with a physical disability to use equipment in practical tasks. ☐

- I use pre-tutoring to improve access to lessons for pupils with learning difficulties – e.g. to introduce and explain subject-specific vocabulary. ☐

- Pupils with disabilities can access technology – e.g. laptops, text to speech software. ☐

- I provide alternatives to written recording for pupils who find writing by hand challenging – e.g. word processing, voice recording. ☐

- I ensure educational visits are made accessible to pupils with disabilities – e.g. by providing additional support or equipment. ☐

A whole school approach to SEN

To *really* ensure the right provision is in place for pupils with SEN, schools need to take a whole school approach to developing their policy and practice. This means senior leaders should be encouraging an ethos which values and respects everyone in the learning community, making the school a place where all learners have an equal right to a high-quality education. In order to do this, schools need to:

1. Ensure any decisions made about provision are informed by the views of the pupils and their parents.

2. Have high ambitions and set challenging targets for pupils with SEN.

3. Carefully track pupils' progress towards these targets and long-term outcomes.

4. Ensure that any approaches used are based on evidence of good practice.

5. Review the impact of any special educational provision on pupil progress.

6. Promote positive outcomes in the wider areas of personal and social development.

Schools must designate an appropriate teacher – the special educational needs coordinator (SENCO) – to take overall responsibility for coordinating provision for pupils with SEN. The role of the SENCO is to work alongside the head teacher and governors to make decisions about SEN developments across the school. The SENCO also coordinates specific provision made to support individual pupils with SEN. Although the SENCO has the overall strategic responsibility and will provide guidance and support to others, meeting the needs of pupils with SEN must be seen as part of *everyone's* role. Ultimately, it is you, the class teacher, who has day-to-day responsibility for ensuring the progress of pupils with SEN.

The graduated approach

As part of the school's overall graduated approach to providing support, HQT must be the first step in responding to pupils who have, or may have, SEN. Chapter 2 details what inclusive HQT looks like. If pupils are receiving HQT but require something additional in order to make progress, the school must try to remove barriers to learning and put effective special educational provision in place through what is known as *SEN support*. This takes the form of a four-part cycle: the assess, plan, do, review cycle. The cycle involves assessing the pupil's needs in detail, agreeing and implementing a plan of action involving additional or targeted support/provision and regularly reviewing the impact of the planned provision on pupil outcomes. The child or young person and their parents should be involved throughout this process, alongside relevant staff from the school: for example, the class teacher, key worker or SENCO. Further information on SEN support and the assess, plan, do, review cycle is given in Chapter 3.

Where a pupil is receiving SEN support and a number of different strategies have been tried but the pupil still isn't making progress, it may be appropriate to involve other professionals. Specialists who work with children and young people with SEN include educational psychologists, speech and language therapists, physiotherapists and school nurses. Specialists can advise on further diagnosis of need and can also provide guidance on effective teaching approaches, resources and interventions to support the pupil's progress. Schools, in agreement with the parents, may involve specialists at any point for advice about a pupil. Chapter 4 provides further information on working in partnership with parents and other professionals.

EHC plans

The provision put in place through SEN support will meet the needs of the majority of children and young people with SEN effectively and enable them to make good progress. For a small minority of those with very significant difficulties however, further provision may be required, due to the complexity of their needs. These pupils may benefit from an EHC plan. This is a legal document that brings the child's education, health and social care needs and provision requirements together into one plan. EHC plans were introduced in 2014 as part of the special educational needs and disability (SEND) reforms and replaced the old statements of SEN (any existing statements will be replaced by 2018).

If an EHC plan is likely to benefit a child or young person, an EHC needs assessment is carried out by the LA, who will make the final decision about whether or not to issue the plan. The LA will work in close partnership with the child, their parents, school and any other professionals involved in supporting the child to draw up the plan. They will gather as much information as possible and, crucially, will consider the views, wishes and feelings of the child and their parents as a key part of the process.

 Did you know?

If an EHC needs assessment is being carried out for a pupil you teach, you may be asked to contribute to the assessment. This will mean providing any relevant information you have on the pupil, including their strengths, needs, the nature and impact of the support you have put in place for them and how well they are meeting the outcomes of any individual learning plan already in place.

In addition to outlining the pupil's needs and provision required, the EHC plan also includes the pupil's views, interests and aspirations, along with the agreed long-term outcomes. The outcomes should be ones that are important to the child and their family, for example being able to live independently or socialise with friends. The EHC plan is an important legal document, so if you have a pupil in your class who has one, check that you have all the information you need in order to implement any aspects of the plan that are relevant to you. It may be useful to discuss the following questions with your SENCO:

- What are the strengths and needs of the pupil?

- What long-term outcomes have been identified in the plan? What are their shorter-term targets?

- What should I be considering when planning my lessons? What strategies should I be using when I am teaching the pupil?

- What additional provision will the pupil receive? What will my role be in delivering/supporting this provision?

- Which other professionals are involved in supporting the pupil? Will I have contact with them?

- How are the pupil's parents involved? When and how should I be communicating with them?

- How should I be monitoring and reviewing the pupil's progress towards the outcomes identified in the plan?

An EHC plan must be reviewed in detail at least once every twelve months to check progress and to see if the plan is still relevant. This is known as the annual review. You will be asked to contribute to this by providing any information you have from your ongoing monitoring and reviewing of the pupil's progress over the year. If you are their class or form tutor, it is likely you will attend the annual review meeting.

 Case study

Eloise, a Year 2 teacher from the East Midlands, describes her involvement in delivering the EHC plan for Barney, a pupil in her class who has ASD:

Once the EHC plan had been finalised, our SENCO arranged a meeting with Barney's mum, our educational psychologist, my teaching assistant and me. We all sat down together and went through each section, discussing the outcomes and checking that everyone understood all aspects of the plan. This was useful because some of the technical information provided by the educational psychologist was explained in more detail and this gave me a better understanding of what makes Barney tick!

We discussed the strategies that would be used with Barney in class and agreed upon which of these strategies would also be useful for mum to try at home. The SENCO asked if my TA would deliver a social skills intervention programme for Barney and three of his peers. Barney came into the meeting towards the end and told us which of his classmates he would like to include. As the intervention was new to my TA, the SENCO agreed to provide some training.

Mum and I now meet on a regular basis to discuss how things are going and I email her most days. We review Barney's support plan three times a year, and the SENCO often comes along to these meetings. Soon it will be the annual review of Barney's EHC plan when we will all be discussing how well his long-term outcomes are being achieved and whether any of the provision outlined in the plan needs reviewing. Most importantly, we will be celebrating all the things Barney has achieved during the year – including becoming best friends with one of his intervention classmates.

Preparing for adulthood

As young people get older, it is important that they are given opportunities to have more control over their lives. All young people need support to successfully go through the transition from childhood to adulthood and this is particularly important for those with SEN. This involves supporting young people with their next steps in life, for example by helping them to make informed choices about whether they will go on to further education, training or employment. It also means enabling young people to be prepared for living independently, being involved in the community and leading healthy lives.

Focused support around preparation for adulthood is particularly important from Year 9 onwards, but should start right from the moment the child or young person is identified as having additional needs. Early years providers and schools can support pupils to be included within social groups and develop friendships as part of their preparation for being involved in the community. As pupils get older, schools can support them by discussing preparation for adulthood in planning and review meetings. They can provide advice and guidance about the options available after pupils have finished their studies. They can help them to prepare for independent living by providing information about housing options and supporting them to find suitable accommodation.

As a class teacher, you may not be directly involved in helping a pupil to make decisions about what they do once they've left your school. However, you can still encourage them to develop aspirations for their future, and support them to become an independent young person, with skills that will make them employable, enable them to participate in their community and help them to understand the value of education.

 Reflect

1. How many pupils have SEN in the class(es) you teach? How does this compare with the national average? What impact does this have on your teaching?

2. Read through the making reasonable adjustments in my classroom list on page 18. Consider which of these adjustments you already make in your classroom and identify any that you don't. Make a plan to put one or two additional adjustments in place over the next few weeks.

3. Do you teach a pupil who has an EHC plan? If so, have another look at the questions on page 22. If you are unsure of the answers to any of these questions, arrange to meet with your SENCO and the pupil, if appropriate, to discuss these points further.

 **Further resources**

The Special Educational Needs and Disability Code of Practice: 0 to 25 Years: www.gov.uk/government/publications/send-code-of-practice-0-to-25.

One of the most useful sections of the Code of Practice is Chapter 6, which provides guidance on the actions schools need to take to ensure they meet their duties towards children and young people with SEN.

Schools: Guide to the 0 to 25 SEND Code of Practice: www.gov.uk/government/uploads/system/uploads/attachment_data/file/349053/Schools_Guide_to_the_0_to_25_SEND_Code_of_Practice.pdf.

A useful guide for SLTs, governors, SENCOs and all classroom teachers on implementing the Code of Practice in schools.

Code of Practice summary: www.nataliepacker.co.uk.

For a briefer summary of the Code of Practice, take a look in the resources section of my website.

The Council for Disabled Children (CDC): www.councilfordisabledchildren.org.uk.

The CDC is the umbrella body for the disabled children's sector in England. Their website contains information on disabled children's rights and resources for pupils, parents, educators and other professionals.

The SEND Gateway: http://www.sendgateway.org.uk.

An online portal for teachers and other education professionals which provides access to lots of free information, resources and training for meeting the needs of children with SEN. The gateway is managed by nasen, the UK's leading organisation for SEN.

Chapter 2
High-quality teaching for all

> High quality teaching, differentiated for individual pupils, is the first step in responding to pupils who have or may have SEN. Additional intervention and support cannot compensate for a lack of good quality teaching.
>
> The Special Educational Needs and Disability Code of Practice, p. 99

In the not too distant past, if you asked teachers the question, 'Who is responsible for pupils with SEN in your school?' the answer would possibly have been 'the SENCO'. Hopefully, this is no longer the case as there is a growing recognition, fuelled by the key messages within the Code of Practice, that all teachers are responsible and accountable for the progress and development of all pupils, including those who have additional needs. Not only is this highlighted in the code, but the Teachers' Standards also require teachers to adapt their practice to respond to the strengths and needs of all pupils.[1] Standard 5 notes that all teachers must:

> have a clear understanding of the needs of all pupils, including those with special educational needs; those of high ability; those with English as an additional language; those with disabilities; and be able to use and evaluate distinctive teaching approaches to engage and support them.
>
> *Teachers' Standards* (2012), p. 12

You are also required to know when and how to differentiate appropriately, to have an understanding of the factors that can inhibit pupils' ability to learn and to demonstrate an awareness of the physical, social and intellectual development of children. That's quite a list, but all these factors underpin quality teaching and learning.

In their 2010 report on the teaching of pupils with SEN, subtitled *A Statement Is Not Enough*, Ofsted noted that the key priority for all

---

1   Department for Education, *Teachers' Standards* (2012). Available at: https://www.education.gov.uk/publications/eOrderingDownload/teachers%20standards.pdf.

children must be 'good teaching and learning'.[2] This may sound like a fairly obvious conclusion, but the Ofsted survey found that some of the most vulnerable pupils in our schools were *not* getting the highest quality teaching and learning and this was resulting in underachievement. The outcomes of this report paved the way for the increased focus on all teachers developing the skills and knowledge necessary to give every pupil the best quality educational experience. Hence, delivering HQT is key to ensuring all pupils, including those with SEN, make good progress.

Did you know?

As part of their overall judgement about a school, Ofsted will take into consideration how well the school is providing for pupils with SEN and disabilities.[3] This involves looking closely at the quality of everyday teaching, learning and assessment for pupils with SEN in addition to any specialist provision they may be receiving.

What is HQT for pupils with SEN?

Inclusive HQT ensures that planning and implementation meets the needs of *all* pupils, and builds in high expectations for *all* pupils, including those with SEN. This is a basic entitlement for every child and young person and should be underpinned by effective whole school teaching and learning policies and frameworks. HQT is about the day-to-day interactions that take place in your classroom and the different pedagogical approaches you use to engage, motivate and challenge learners. It is about the way you use assessment and feedback to identify gaps and help

---

2   Ofsted, *The Special Educational Needs and Disability Review: A Statement Is Not Enough* (2010). Ref: 090221. Available at: https://www.gov.uk/government/uploads/system/uploads/attachment_data/file/413814/Special_education_needs_and_disability_review.pdf.

3   Ofsted, *School Inspection Handbook* (2015). Ref: 150066. Available at: https://www.gov.uk/government/publications/school-inspection-handbook-from-september-2015.

pupils to move on in their learning. It is about providing both support and challenge in order to enable pupils to achieve more.

On a practical level, HQT involves the teacher drawing on a range of strategies that are closely matched to the learning objectives of the lesson (which, in turn, will match the particular learning needs of the pupils in the class). However, the real 'test' of whether HQT is in place is not necessarily what the teaching includes, but what the pupils achieve (i.e. the learning outcomes!). As a result of inclusive HQT, pupils with SEN will:

- Be engaged and motivated to learn.

- Enjoy their learning and rise to the challenge.

- Know where they are in their learning, where they need to go next and how to get there.

- Become independent and resilient.

- Develop skills, knowledge and understanding across a range of areas.

- Recognise they have made progress with their learning from their own starting point.

So what elements of teaching are most likely to lead to these outcomes and what does an inclusive lesson look like? We can think about a lesson as being a bit like a jigsaw that contains many different pieces, each one links in some way to several others. The jigsaw diagram below outlines nine elements of HQT for pupils with SEN. This is not to suggest there are *only* nine elements to a good quality, inclusive lesson, but those identified here are key. If one or more of these pieces are missing, the lesson is likely to be incomplete. When we tackle a jigsaw, we often start by identifying the corner pieces. In our HQT diagram, the corners are the foundations that need to come first – they are the elements that the lesson is built upon: for example, we have to know our pupils well before we can plan to engage and challenge them. The piece in the middle of the jigsaw – developing independence – completes the picture and is the final piece of the puzzle. Ultimately, our aim as teachers is to develop children and young people who are independent thinkers and learners.

HQT for pupils with SEN

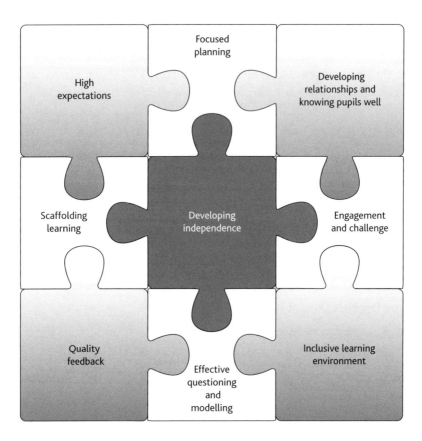

Some of the pieces in the HQT jigsaw refer to ways in which we might differentiate our lessons: for example, we might use different types of questioning with particular pupils or vary the amount of scaffolding we provide for individuals. The purpose of differentiation is to enable all pupils to achieve by making learning accessible while always providing a high level of challenge and expectation. It is about anticipating the needs of all pupils and motivating them to succeed. This can only be done if we have a good understanding of where the pupil is in their learning, so we can plan from *their* starting point. In essence, it is about personalising learning, and this is a phrase that some educationalists prefer to use instead of the term differentiation.

Being a reflective practitioner, it is helpful to take time to consider how *you* (the teacher) effectively implement each of the pieces of the jigsaw. However, you also have a responsibility to consider how other adults in your classroom support these elements of HQT. Deploying TAs or other adults effectively in order to move pupils' learning on is a key aspect of inclusive HQT and is covered in detail in Chapter 4.

High expectations

If there is one thing that is likely to make a huge difference to the impact you have on all your pupils, it's having high expectations. Studies by Rosenthal and Jacobson showed that the higher the expectations teachers had of their pupils, the better they performed.[4] The 2010 Ofsted SEND review also concluded that high aspirations (along with a focus on developing independence) led to the best achievement for those with SEN.[5]

Put simply, high expectations are key to success, but unfortunately, those high expectations are not always evident. In her book, *Assessment for Learning without Limits*, Dame Alison Peacock talks about the potential problem that can occur 'when false, limiting assumptions are made about children's capacity to learn'.[6] Although it's unlikely you would ever hear a teacher say that they *didn't* have high expectations for their pupils, they can sometimes have 'hidden' low expectations of certain pupils (for example, those who find learning challenging and have lower prior attainment). When ability grouping is used, for example, research by the Education Endowment Foundation (EEF) has shown that pupils' confidence can be undermined if they are placed in lower sets: the belief that attainment can be improved through effort can often be unintentionally undermined.[7] Continually setting lower level learning challenges for

---

4   See Robert Rosenthal and Lenore Jacobson, Teachers' expectancies: Determinants of pupils' IQ gains, *Psychological Reports* (1966), 19: 115–118. Available at: http://www.indiana.edu/~educy520/readings/rosenthal66.pdf.

5   Ofsted, *Special Educational Needs And Disability Review*, pp. 6–7.

6   Alison Peacock, *Assessment for Learning without Limits* (London: Open University Press, 2016), p. 51.

7   Education Endowment Foundation, Teaching and Learning Toolkit. Available at: https://educationendowmentfoundation.org.uk/resources/teaching-learning-toolkit/setting-or-streaming/.

particular groups or individuals can put a ceiling on what we think they can achieve. Inclusive teaching is about moving *all* pupils forward without limiting their learning.

Having high expectations starts with the belief that every child can succeed and communicating this belief to every child. However, teachers who demonstrate high expectations for their pupils do not simply *tell* them that they have high expectations for them: they consistently *show* them. While the reality is that not all pupils will meet the standards all the time, you need to aim for excellence by setting an ambitious goal and then supporting each pupil to constantly work towards that goal. This means, for example, expecting a pupil to use precise technical vocabulary, even if they have language difficulties, or providing feedback that is positive, yet expresses the expectation that the pupil needs to go further with their learning – for example, 'You've found the first two possible solutions, can you now find the last one?'

As well as having high expectations of your pupils yourself, you should insist that your pupils have high expectations of themselves. Children will only make improvements in their learning if they believe in themselves. For those who find learning a constant struggle (and think their peers are making more progress than they are), getting them to do this can be quite a challenge. Model and encourage a growth mindset, so pupils believe that they can improve if they work hard.[8] This means never settling for work that is less than their best, setting aspirational goals for themselves and practising over and over again. Teach pupils that challenge is positive and that the ability to overcome challenge will help them become successful learners.

---

8   For more on growth mindset, see Carol Dweck, *Mindset: The New Psychology of Success* (New York: Ballantine Books, 2006).

Try it!

3 B4 Me

To encourage pupils to overcome challenges when they get stuck with their learning, try introducing the 3 B4 Me strategy. Before a pupil goes to an adult for help they must try the following:

1.   **B**rain (think for themselves).

2.   **B**uddy (ask a peer).

3.   **B**ook or **b**oard (use classroom resources).

Developing relationships and knowing pupils well

HQT and learning is fundamentally underpinned by quality relationships. The importance of developing positive relationships with all your pupils cannot be underestimated. Make sure you are well-informed about the pupils you teach and that you know them as individuals. Find out not only what their needs are but also what their strengths are and what interests or motivates them. Some pupils will have personal circumstances that impact significantly on their ability to concentrate or learn: they may be caring for family members, they may be subject to domestic violence or they may have recently suffered loss. Showing empathy can go a long way: let them know that you have their best interests at heart and that you *like* them (this is really important, even if it may be a challenge with certain individuals!).

Phoebe, a Year 11 student who has complex physical needs and suffers from anxiety, says:

> Just knowing that one teacher sometimes thinks about me and makes the effort to ask if I've had a good day or what my weekend was like

does make a difference. It's like they know I exist and they're interested in me as a person.

A good place to start is to look at the pupil's individual support plan (ISP) (e.g. their Pupil Passport or profile). The plan should provide you with information on their needs and strengths and may also give targets and suggested strategies to use when teaching. Take a look at their work and speak to previous teachers, the SENCO, TAs, parents and, most importantly, the pupil to find out what they're really like and what helps them to learn.

Use any data you have been given, or the outcomes of any assessments you've done, to gain a sound understanding of where your pupils are in their learning. This information will be essential when you start planning lessons and will also help you set appropriate targets for individuals. Depending on need, these targets might not only focus on academic areas, but could include more holistic ones such as personal and social skills, physical skills or independence. Ongoing assessment of learning will be crucial to ensure you continue to know each of your pupils as well as you possibly can. Further information on assessment is given in Chapter 3.

 Case study

Charlotte Jackson, a teacher in the early stages of her career, explains how she got to know her first class well:

> During my NQT year I was lucky enough to work at a school for pupils with complex needs, many of whom were autistic. I prepared for my new role by reading as much as I could about ASD. However, when I met my KS1 class, it immediately became apparent that while some of the 'typical' characteristics were evident in some pupils, they all had very different, and individual, needs. In addition to their assessment data, the information I received about each child simply by chatting to their previous teacher and my TA was invaluable. The pupil profiles and individual learning plans gave me details on their strengths, areas of difficulty, targets and strategies, along with important dos and don'ts. (One child had a strong aversion to the colour red, so I knew I had to choose my work clothes carefully!) I also used some of my NQT time to just observe my

pupils and note the way they interacted with others around them, which was really useful.

Inclusive learning environment

Developing relationships in order to get to know your pupils is part of creating a positive environment for learning, as is setting up a classroom that is welcoming, safe and nurturing. Here pupils will feel secure and will not be afraid to take risks with their learning. They will respect the strengths and needs of others and recognise the value of everyone's contribution.

In her book, *How to Be an Amazing Teacher*, education adviser and consultant Caroline Bentley-Davies refers to the classroom climate and asks teachers, 'What is the weather like in your classroom?'[9] This is a useful analogy, as the way you express your feelings and attitudes and the mood you create sets the atmosphere, or ambiance, in your class. If you're happy, upbeat and enthusiastic to learn, it's more likely that your pupils will be too! For some of our most vulnerable pupils, being at school can be the most positive (and safest) part of their day. It is therefore our moral duty to ensure they have a positive experience when they are with us.

When you look around your classroom environment:

- Is it welcoming? Does it encourage more reluctant pupils to want to be there and to learn?

- Is it well-organised and tidy? Is it supportive of pupils for whom a well-structured and orderly environment is important?

- Are there attractive and accessible displays that help learning and celebrate pupils' work? Is the work of *all* pupils included?

- Have you used the information you've gathered about your pupils to consider the seating plan? Are pupils who might be easily

---

9   Caroline Bentley-Davies, *How to Be an Amazing Teacher* (Carmarthen: Crown House Publishing, 2010), p. 45.

distracted sat away from windows, heaters or peers who talk too much?

- Are you using any available outdoor learning environment as an extension of the classroom? Can all pupils access this effectively?

- Are pupils encouraged to take responsibility for their environment? Are pupils who have difficulty with organisation supported to do this effectively?

Your classroom environment can also help with behaviour management. If the room is calm and orderly, the behaviour of those spending time in it (including you!) is more likely to also be calm and orderly. Establishing clear and consistent rules and systems in your class is essential for all pupils, but will be especially helpful for pupils with particular needs, including those with ASD or ADHD.

 Try it!

Work station

Consider creating a distraction-free learning area in your room for pupils to use if they need to move away from their peers or from other stimuli. Try setting up a work station, which is essentially a table surrounded by screens to minimise visual distractions. This can be particularly useful for some pupils with ASD or others who have difficulty concentrating in busy environments.

Setting up an inclusive classroom also means having a range of resources readily available for all pupils to use independently. Early years environments are full of practical equipment that children can choose to use to learn with and explore. However, many older pupils with SEN will continue to benefit from using hands-on resources such as:

- visuals (word mats, visual timetables, symbols, photographs)

- manipulatives (counters, number squares, objects, artefacts)

- timers (clocks, hourglasses, stopwatches)

- reading trackers

- sensory materials (sand, rice, mud, shaving foam)

- assistive technology tools

When choosing new resources for your classroom, don't forget to consider how they will support pupils in their learning, how you will ensure pupils use the resources effectively and how the resources will empower pupils to become more independent.

Quality feedback

Feedback is verbal or written information given to the pupil and/or the teacher about a pupil's performance in order to improve learning. It can be about the learning activity itself, the process, the pupil's management of their learning or them as individuals. Research by John Hattie shows that improving the quality of feedback in the classroom can have a significant impact on learning.[10] However, the same research suggests it can have a negative effect if not used well! It is therefore important to understand what makes good feedback and how it can be used to particular effect with pupils who find learning challenging.

When providing feedback to pupils with SEN, consider the following points:

- Check that pupils clearly understand the learning objective and success criteria for the lesson. Provide some visual prompts that they can refer to when self-assessing.

- Be specific, accurate and clear with your feedback – for example, 'I especially like how you have included a question in the opening paragraph', rather than 'That's an excellent story starter, well done!' Provide specific guidance on their next steps rather than simply highlighting errors.

---

10 See John Hattie, *Visible Learning for Teachers: Maximising Impact on Learning* (Abingdon: Routledge, 2012).

- Use verbal praise carefully so that it is meaningful and does not overwhelm the learner. For some pupils, praise will help their self-esteem and motivation, but give too much praise and they soon start to sense a lack of sincerity! Remember that some pupils may not be comfortable with verbal feedback in front of their peers, so be discreet.

- Pupils can become demotivated if someone else picks up a lot of mistakes in their work. Be selective with what you ask them to correct (particularly with spellings) and emphasise the importance of effort and perseverance.

- Some pupils may find it difficult to reflect on their learning. Teach pupils specific skills for self- and peer assessing, such as marking their work against success criteria. For some pupils with slower processing speeds, extra time might be needed to respond to feedback.

Through these approaches, you will be able to make ongoing, well-founded judgements about each individual's progress, identify any misconceptions or gaps in learning and use this to inform the next stages of learning and planning.

Focused planning

The curriculum offer in your school needs to be one that caters for the needs of all pupils, including those with SEND. The majority of pupils will be able to follow the national curriculum, where this is applicable.[11] The national curriculum emphasises the importance of setting suitable learning challenges for all pupils, responding to pupils' needs and over-coming potential barriers for individuals or groups of pupils. As well as having high expectations and setting ambitious targets, teachers need to set suitable learning challenges for pupils in order to effectively plan lessons for all. In their book *Teaching Backwards*, Andy Griffith and Mark

---

11 Department for Education, *The National Curriculum in England Framework Document* (2013). Available at: https://www.gov.uk/government/uploads/system/uploads/attachment_data/file/210969/NC_framework_document_-_FINAL.pdf.

Burns introduce the concept of backwards planning.[12] This model refers to a planning journey that starts with the end in mind. The backwards planning process can provide much greater clarity for both the teacher and the pupils. When developing lessons, consider the following, based on the backwards planning model:

1. **Establish the starting point of each learner.**

   Consider: How well do you know your pupils as individuals? Is the starting point for pupils with SEN similar to others in the class? If not, how will you accommodate this? Are there gaps in their learning? How can you build on their strengths and interests?

2. **Identify the desired result.**

   Consider: What knowledge, skills or understanding do you want pupils to make progress with? For pupils with SEN, is there a need to reinforce basic literacy or numeracy skills? How will you ensure pupils with cognitive difficulties understand the learning outcomes?

3. **Determine what will prove understanding.**

   Consider: How will you know if the learning objectives have been met? What are your success criteria? For pupils with SEN, are smaller-step criteria required for them to achieve success?

4. **Plan learning experiences.**

   Consider: How will you ensure the learning activities are accessed by pupils with SEN and/or disabilities? Are any specialist resources required for individuals? How will you assess and monitor the progress of all pupils, including those with SEN?

Many pupils with cognitive difficulties will prefer lessons that have structure and break down learning into small steps. Try planning short tasks and varied activities that will hold pupils' attention and keep them interested. Use concrete approaches to explain new concepts and don't

---

12 Andy Griffith and Mark Burns, *Teaching Backwards* (Carmarthen: Crown House Publishing, 2014).

forget that pupils will benefit from teaching approaches that make links with their own everyday experiences.

Engagement and challenge

What you do in the first few minutes of a lesson to really engage pupils is crucial. The opening to the lesson starts pupils off on the right track, prepares them for learning and gets them into 'flow'. This is the state described by Mihaly Csikszentmihali when a person is so focused on an activity they are engaged in, time seems to disappear and distractions don't get a chance to enter their thoughts.[13] Flow occurs in the classroom when a learner is given an activity with a high level of challenge, but where they have the right level of skill to tackle that challenge. Getting this balance just right for all the learners in your class can be tricky – this partly comes down to knowing your pupils (again!) and understanding that some will need more time and support to embed the basic skills for learning.

For pupils who have difficulty focusing, it's essential to get them into flow as soon as possible. Have an activity for them to start as soon as they come into the lesson. This might be a puzzle, card sort activity, cloze procedure (an activity in which words are omitted from a piece of text and pupils fill in the blanks) or open-ended question such as, 'How many ways can you find to make the number 21?' Try planning an activity that either reinforces the learning from a previous lesson or links to the learning in the lesson you are about to deliver. Make sure the activity is one that all pupils can access and begin without too much input from an adult (i.e. an activity for which they already have the required skills).

---

13 Mihaly Csikszentmihali, *Flow: The Psychology of Optimal Experience* (New York: Harper and Row, 1990).

Try it!

Picture perfect

As a starter activity, on the board show an interesting picture or photograph that relates to the topic of the lesson and ask pupils to:

1. Label what they can see in the picture.

2. Infer three pieces of information from the picture.

3. Think of three questions they would like to ask to find out more about the picture.

For pupils who may struggle with devising questions, provide question starter prompts to help them. Take a look at http://www.literacyshed.com/the-images-shed.html for some examples of really great images.

Engaging activities should get pupils thinking and start challenging them right away. If the task is too easy, the pupils learn nothing. If the task is too difficult, pupils are unlikely to experience any success and will become demotivated. For those with SEN, the nature of the task is particularly important because the outcome may affect motivation and self-esteem. The trick is to get the right balance of tasks that are achievable *and* that will provide challenge. Pupils need to feel confident that the task isn't impossible, so you may want to chunk tasks so they get incrementally more difficult.

Challenge requires pupils to apply their knowledge, skills and experience. When planning for challenge, you need to feel confident that pupils have developed the appropriate knowledge and skills in the first place. For example, if you are asking a pupil to solve a mathematical word problem, do they have the skills required to tackle the relevant calculations within it, and the ability to read the word problem itself?

Challenge often encourages a range of creative solutions, not necessarily just one right answer. Providing open-ended tasks that give pupils the opportunity to find different routes through their learning, or present their learning in different ways, can be a useful way to introduce challenge. For pupils who have relatively fixed thought processes, however, the idea that there could be more than one 'right answer' can be tricky to grasp. Check that pupils understand this at the start of the task, and provide a couple of examples to demonstrate the point.

Effective questioning and modelling

Questioning is central to developing our thinking and our capacity to learn. Skilful questioning in the classroom is one of the most powerful tools available to you, as it makes the thinking process visible (and can be a great way to provide challenge). However, it's not always easy to do and, too often, teachers' questioning focuses on factual recall and other lower order type information. It is a common misunderstanding that if a pupil has cognitive difficulties they should be focusing on lower order questions. Although these types of questions are important, we need to ensure all pupils have opportunities to respond to, and develop, higher order questions that involve analysis, evaluation or creation. When you know a pupil well you can target your questions and consider the best way to introduce higher level questioning for challenge.

 Did you know?

According to some estimates, on average, teachers give pupils only 1.5 seconds of 'wait-time' to answer a question before moving on – not very long at all, especially for a pupil with processing difficulties![14] When waiting time is increased, the likelihood of getting a response also increases and the quality and depth of answers improves.

It doesn't matter how well-structured and challenging your questions are if a pupil chooses not to respond. Some pupils who are shy or have low

---

14 Mary Budd Rowe, Wait Time: Slowing Down May Be a Way of Speeding Up, *American Educator* 11 (Spring 1987): 38–43, 47. EJ 351 827.

self-esteem may not want to answer questions aloud, while some can be so keen they don't give others a chance! All pupils should be expected to be involved in responding to questions and also need to be taught how to develop effective questions of their own. This begins with creating a classroom environment where pupils feel safe to take risks and know they won't be ridiculed for giving inaccurate responses.

 Try it!

I'll get back to you

If a pupil has difficulty processing information and takes a long time to respond to questions as a result, ask them a question and tell them you will give them three or four minutes to think about it and come back to them (don't forget to return to them once the time is up!). If the pupil then replies with 'I don't know' suggest they 'phone a friend' by nominating someone else to answer. Make sure the pupil still contributes by stating whether or not they agree with their friend's response or by building on it further.

Show pupils how to respond to questions, solve problems and complete tasks by modelling this first. Modelling refers to the teacher (or another adult or pupil) demonstrating the process and end product before pupils are expected to try it themselves. It is an essential method of teaching and a fundamental means by which pupils with cognitive difficulties learn: through observing what is expected. As part of your planning process, clarify in your own mind the elements of a learning task or process you think a pupil with specific needs might struggle with and plan the best way to model this for them. There are many ways to model, including shared writing, using past exam papers or showing exemplar WAGOLLs (What A Good One Looks Like) or WABOLLs (What A Bad One Looks Like).

The psychologist Lev Vygotsky noted that children learn to think most effectively by talking to others.[15] Through dialogue, children can explore

---

15 See http://www.simplypsychology.org/vygotsky.html.

and refine their ideas and share their understanding, which in turn will help them to make better sense of it. Ensure pupils have regular opportunities to engage in conversation about their learning and develop their thinking through discussion. For pupils who find learning a challenge, the process of talking to help them self-scaffold their thinking can be particularly effective. While you are doing any modelling, remember to talk through the key steps or procedures. Give pupils opportunities to join in gradually so you can guide their thinking before they have a go independently. Modelling the writing process, for example, can have a particularly positive impact on those pupils who struggle to take on the thinking processes of a competent writer.

Scaffolding learning

Scaffolding involves using a range of strategies to provide temporary support for pupils, encouraging them to think of their own problem solving strategies and moving them towards being more independent. Just like the physical scaffolding we might see on a building, learning scaffolds are gradually removed when they are no longer needed: the teacher shifts more responsibility for learning over to the pupil. Scaffolding can be used to bridge learning gaps and prevent pupils becoming frustrated or discouraged when they don't yet have the requisite skills to tackle an activity independently.

Scaffolding occurs through careful observation of what a pupil is doing, asking questions to check the pupil's understanding and then providing structured help while enabling the pupil to do as much as possible themselves. Practical ways you can scaffold learning include:

- Using visual clues to help pupils understand instructions, tasks or text.

- Providing instructions one or two at a time, or giving pupils a checklist of instructions they can tick off as they complete each one.

- Pre-highlighting the most important aspects of a text so pupils know which parts to focus on.

- Providing sentence starters for discussion or writing.

- Showing models for pupils to compare with their own work.

- Using graphic organisers, such as mind maps or writing frames so pupils have a structure for recording their ideas.

Another useful way of scaffolding is to provide support with reading, understanding and using keywords, or subject-specific vocabulary. Keywords are those words that are of central importance to a subject or topic: learning to use them can be particularly tricky for pupils with cognitive or speech and language difficulties. Provide a keyword mat or list of keywords with definitions. Alternatively, show examples of how the keywords can be used in sentences as this helps to contextualise the language and provides a model for pupils to follow.

 Try it!

Keyword Pictionary

On a piece of card, write a keyword that you want pupils to focus on for the lesson. Pupils work in pairs. One of the pair takes the card and, without their partner seeing the word, has to try to draw a representation of the word. Their partner has to guess what the word is from the drawing.

Developing independence

One of our ultimate goals as teachers should be to enable pupils to become independent thinkers and independent learners (in essence, our job is to make ourselves redundant!). This means pupils having an understanding of their learning, being motivated to take responsibility for it and taking control of it. Some pupils with SEN are given a huge amount of adult support at school and can become rather dependent on others, so developing independence is even more of a priority for them.

When we promote independent learning we are enabling our pupils to become self-directed in their learning experiences and to have more autonomy and control over their learning behaviour. Key aspects of being an independent learner include the ability to think about the learning process, make choices, reflect, ask for support when needed, develop research skills and be accountable for learning. How can we support pupils to develop these essential skills?

- Teach pupils a range of strategies they can use if they get stuck with their learning (for example, 3 B4 Me). Ensure any resources needed are accessible and clearly organised.

- Encourage pupils to take risks with their learning and understand that failure is part of the learning process. This can be particularly difficult for pupils to understand if they have a fixed way of thinking: explicitly model how to handle any associated negative feelings or behaviours.

- Enable individuals to take the lead in some lessons – e.g. by teaching a peer or being the 'expert' in a particular topic (this is really useful when a pupil has a particular interest or skill).

- Encourage pupils to reflect on their learning. Provide opportunities for them to talk through their learning processes, share how they solved problems and explain which strategies they used. Developing these metacognitive skills (thinking about thinking) will support pupils to become more effective learners.

 Case study

Hannah Ogden, a recently qualified history and geography teacher at Guiseley School encourages her learners to be independent:

> As I progress in teaching, I am becoming more confident in using the strategy of allowing pupils choice and giving them responsibility within their learning. At first this seemed quite daunting and risky as it felt like I was relinquishing control. However, I have begun to ask pupils how confident they are with a topic and encourage them to choose their own 'starting point' activity. By having

different challenge-level tasks or resources around the room for pupils to access, I can spend more time questioning, explaining and discussing elements with the least confident, as well as being able to carry out ongoing assessment of all pupils. Pupils can upgrade or downgrade their challenge once they begin, depending on how easy or hard they find it and I can advise them on this too. Not only have I found this a great way for pupils to learn, it is also helping to develop independence and resilience within all learners, which I consider to be one of my key responsibilities as a teacher.

Remember that the elements highlighted in the HQT jigsaw on page 30 are not the only aspects of HQT for pupils with SEN and there will be others you can identify. Considering the pieces in the jigsaw, and any of your own ideas, ask yourself: are these different to what makes HQT for *any* pupil? The answer should be a resounding no! What we are referring to here is simply good teaching that meets the needs of *all* pupils and enables *all* pupils to make progress in their learning.

 Case study

The following example illustrates how Sarah March, an English teacher at St James' Catholic High School in Barnet, uses a range of strategies to ensure high-quality teaching for her Year 10 class. The group includes a number of students who have a wide range of additional needs.

The class have recently been studying *Lord of the Flies*. In one lesson, pupils were learning to understand the importance of different places on the island. As soon as they walked into the classroom, pupils were provided with an engaging activity relating to their own personal experience. A floor plan of the school was shown on the board and pupils were asked to decide where in the school was important to them and why. They wrote their individual responses on sticky notes and placed them in the corresponding place on the floor plan.

In order for students to recap prior learning, Sarah used visual and auditory clues to help them recall some of the key aspects of the story – pictures and pieces of music represented particular places on the island. Pupils were then asked to identify positive and negative responses to the places and find direct quotes from the text to back up and justify their responses. This activity was done in small groups and recording was done on a large group map. Clear verbal instructions were given and, for some pupils, these were also written on whiteboards for them to refer back to if needed. Keywords were highlighted or underlined.

The two TAs not only worked alongside pupils with very complex needs but supported the whole class by prompting, emphasising key vocabulary, assessing understanding through questioning, following up any misunderstandings and encouraging pupils to justify answers.

Sarah used mini-plenaries throughout the lesson to review and consolidate learning and, at the end, used the 'Exit Card' strategy. She provided an A5 template and pupils recorded a summary of their key learning, noting what they had achieved and any next steps in learning.

Throughout the lesson, Sarah outlined her high expectations for behaviour and quality of work and ensured all pupils worked towards meeting these expectations. The series of short, focused, practical activities kept pupils on task throughout and careful questioning from all the adults gave pupils the opportunity to think at a deeper level. Feedback from pupils highlighted the progress they had made with their learning as a result of the strategies and techniques Sarah used. Pupils also commented on how much they had enjoyed the lesson.

Reflect

1. Have another look at the HQT jigsaw on page 30. Which of the aspects are strengths of your teaching? Can you identify one or two of the areas that you could develop further?

2. How effectively do you provide feedback to pupils with cognitive difficulties? What strategies do you use to gain feedback from them about their learning?

3. Consider a lesson you are about to plan. What are some of the practical ways you can ensure HQT for your pupils with particular learning needs in this lesson?

Further resources

Assessment for Learning without Limits, Alison Peacock

Inspirational stories of formative assessment in practice showing how children can achieve when there are no limits to their learning.

How to Be an Amazing Teacher, Caroline Bentley-Davies

Tips, techniques and tactics for becoming a great primary or secondary teacher.

Engaging Learners, Andy Griffith and Mark Burns

Guidance on how to develop intrinsic motivation in learners to develop independent learning and creativity and improve behaviour management.

Visible Learning for Teachers, John Hattie

A summary of the largest meta-analysis of research into what actually works (and what doesn't work) in schools to improve learning.

Teaching and Learning Toolkit, Education Endowment Foundation: https://educationendowmentfoundation.org.uk/toolkit/toolkit-a-z/.

A summary of educational research which provides guidance for teachers and schools on how to use their resources to improve attainment. Each topic is summarised in terms of average impact on attainment, the strength of the supporting evidence and cost.

Chapter 3
Successful SEN support

Teachers are responsible and accountable for the progress and development of the pupils in their class, including where pupils access support from teaching assistants or specialist staff.

The Special Educational Needs and Disability Code of Practice, p. 99

What is SEN support?

So you're feeling confident that your classroom reflects an inclusive environment, you have high expectations and encourage independence. You know your pupils well, plan engaging and challenging lessons and provide quality feedback. However, despite the fact you seem to have all the pieces of the HQT jigsaw in place, there are still some individuals who are struggling to make progress. What do you do next?

Pupils who continue to face challenges in their learning, despite receiving HQT, are likely to need additional strategies, or different provision, in order to meet their needs. The Code of Practice states that, for these pupils, teachers are required to remove barriers to learning and put effective special educational provision in place through SEN support. This SEN support takes the form of a four-part cycle (assess, plan, do, review). Through this cycle, actions are reviewed and refined as understanding of a pupil's needs and the support required to help them secure good outcomes increases. This is known as the graduated approach.

Did you know?

Guidance on the graduated approach is provided in Chapter 6 of the Code of Practice. However, there is flexibility built in to the code to allow schools to implement SEN support in the way they feel is best for their pupils. This means there will be slightly different practice in your school to that seen in other schools around the country – for example, in the terminology used to describe the graduated approach.

Whole school assessment and tracking

The graduated approach is at the heart of good whole school practice, starting with HQT and effective assessment, tracking and monitoring. Initially, the graduated approach involves you using the information you gather from your ongoing, day-to-day assessment to make judgements about the progress a pupil is making and to alert you to any barriers that may be getting in the way of them making comparable progress to their peers. This information might come from questioning the pupil, marking their work, discussing their work with them or from the outcomes of short assessment tasks. You will also get valuable information from observing the pupil (in lessons and in less structured situations) or having discussions with parents, other members of staff or the pupil. The information can then be used to answer the following questions:

■ In what areas of the curriculum is the pupil doing well? In what areas are they struggling?

■ What are the pupil's current levels of attainment and how do these compare with expected levels of attainment?

■ What progress has the pupil made over the term or year? Is this at least expected progress?

- Is the pupil on track to achieve their end of term/year/key stage targets?

- If the pupil has been involved in targeted intervention, have they made accelerated progress?

- What does this information tell us about the pupil's confidence and attitude to learning?

- What are the pupil's views on their learning?

Remember that, due to the nature of their barriers to learning, some pupils with cognitive difficulties may not be able to reach age-related expectations of attainment, no matter how much support and intervention is provided. However, the majority of pupils should still be able to make progress from their starting point. You should therefore be seeking to identify pupils who are making less than expected progress given their age and individual barriers to learning. Less than expected progress is characterised in the Code of Practice as progress which:

- is significantly slower than that of their peers starting from the same baseline

- fails to match or better the child's previous rate of progress

- fails to close the attainment gap between the child and their peers

- widens the attainment gap[1]

This shouldn't, however, be restricted to progress in English, maths and other academic subjects. If a pupil is struggling to make progress in their communication, social skills, behaviour, emotional health or physical development, then identifying and meeting these needs is equally important. Assessing pupils' skills in these areas can be tricky; however, there are a range of ways this can be done. Your SENCO should be able to provide support with ways of measuring progress in the wider curriculum.

---

1   DfE (2014), *Special Educational Needs and Disability Code of Practice*, p. 95.

Identifying the need

If you continue to have concerns about progress but the pupil has not previously been identified as having SEN, your next step is to talk to the SENCO. During this discussion, show examples of any information you have gathered (as outlined previously) and evidence of what HQT strategies you have already put in place, as well as any impact these have had. This will demonstrate you are being proactive. Some schools will have an 'initial concerns' sheet for teachers to complete to record all this information to share during the discussion with the SENCO. Don't forget to include the outcomes of any conversations you have had with the pupil and their parents. The evidence about the pupil's lack of progress may lead to a decision, taken jointly by the SENCO, you the teacher and the parents, to place the pupil on the school's SEN register or record because they require some kind of additional, special educational provision.

 Did you know?

When it is decided that a child requires SEN support, the school must formally notify the child's parents. This is a statutory requirement and every school should have a procedure in place for this to happen.

It can be tempting to 'label' a pupil as soon as concerns are raised; on many occasions, teachers or parents have been heard saying something along the lines of, 'This child has difficulty with reading and spelling, therefore they must be dyslexic.' However, it's not always appropriate or useful to label children in this way. Furthermore, as a class teacher you cannot be expected to identify every condition known (and, to be honest, we shouldn't expect the SENCO to be able to do this either, as skilled and knowledgeable as they are!). It is, however, useful to have knowledge of some of the common areas of need you are likely to come across, which is where Part 2 of this book can help.

If a pupil has been identified as having SEN, then additional and increasingly personalised support or provision is required through SEN support and the four-stage cycle. In the past, implementing this sort of cycle might have been seen as the responsibility of the SENCO. However, the Code of Practice makes it clear that this cycle is for teachers and that they have a key role to play in each of the stages.

The assess, plan, do, review cycle

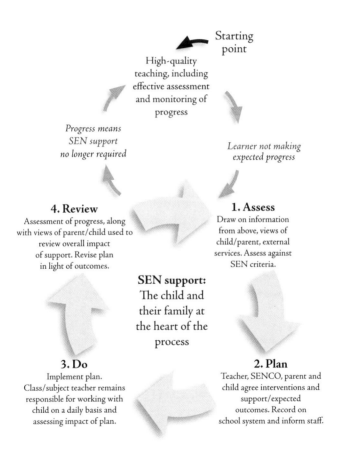

Starting point

High-quality teaching, including effective assessment and monitoring of progress

Progress means SEN support no longer required

Learner not making expected progress

4. Review
Assessment of progress, along with views of parent/child used to review overall impact of support. Revise plan in light of outcomes.

1. Assess
Draw on information from above, views of child/parent, external services. Assess against SEN criteria.

SEN support:
The child and their family at the heart of the process

3. Do
Implement plan. Class/subject teacher remains responsible for working with child on a daily basis and assessing impact of plan.

2. Plan
Teacher, SENCO, parent and child agree interventions and support/expected outcomes. Record on school system and inform staff.

Assess

The assess stage starts with teachers using the information they gather as part of the whole school assessment process (as outlined previously) to make judgements about the progress a pupil is making. Once again, knowing the pupil well and having a really clear understanding of the gaps in their learning and the potential barriers is crucial to enable you to plan effective teaching and determine appropriate provision.

On occasions, in addition to the ongoing formative assessments and regular summative information gathered as part of the whole school approach, a pupil may need to be assessed in more detail in order to explore the precise gaps in their learning or to move towards a formal diagnosis, if appropriate. Depending on the exact nature of the assessments required, this is likely to be something the SENCO arranges and could include:

- Standardised reading, spelling or maths tests.

- Other diagnostic assessments, such as verbal and non-verbal reasoning tests.

- Use of profiling tools to identify detailed needs – e.g. for SLCN.

- Observation schedules.

- Screening assessments – e.g. for dyslexia or dyspraxia.

- Request for advice from a specialist professional, such as an educational psychologist, speech therapist, social worker or health professional.

Further discussions with the pupil and their parents will also be invaluable at this point. This will enable you or the SENCO to gather more detailed information on the pupil's home life, what the pupil is like outside school, the pupil's views on school and learning or strategies the parents use at home to support their child. Where there is likely to be an impact on teaching and learning, a summary of the outcomes of any additional assessments should be shared with you to support your planning.

Did you know?

Some schools use cognitive abilities tests (CATs) to assess their pupils. These tests can measure a range of cognitive abilities such as verbal reasoning, non-verbal reasoning, numerical reasoning, spatial ability and abstract reasoning. The outcomes of the assessments can be used to identify a pupil's strengths, weaknesses and learning preferences.

Plan

This part of the cycle involves discussing, planning and agreeing what will be put in place as an outcome of the assessment information gathered. The planning should involve the pupil, parents and staff from the school who know the pupil well. In a primary school this is likely to be the class teacher, with support from the SENCO if appropriate. In a secondary school this could be the form tutor, key worker, SENCO or another member of the SEN team. Where other professionals are working with the child, they should also contribute to planning.

The initial step of the planning process should include agreeing targets for the pupil in order to focus attention on key areas and give them a clear idea of what they need to do to improve their work. The targets can also help parents to know how to support their child's learning. They will also enable you to evaluate the effectiveness of your teaching strategies. The targets should aim to support the pupil to work towards their identified long-term outcomes. Depending on the needs of the pupil, targets might have an academic focus: for example, 'I will know my number bonds to 20', or relate to other areas of need, such as personal or organisational skills: for example, 'I will remember to bring my full PE kit to school every Tuesday and Friday'.

When establishing what support is required to enable the pupil to meet their identified targets, the first step should be to ensure HQT is in place and agree any adjustments that you might need to make. Following this, additional or targeted support should be identified, along with any specific teaching strategies, approaches or specialist resources to be used. This might include:

- specialist programmes or a personalised curriculum

- additional resources

- working in a small group – e.g. a nurture group

- peer support

- extra support from an adult

- physical or personal care support

- targeted interventions to focus on key skills

Where additional targeted provision is planned for, there should be clear and expected outcomes linked directly to the provision. Any targeted interventions should be delivered by staff who have the appropriate skills and knowledge. A timescale for reviewing the plan, and details of how progress will be monitored, also needs to be agreed.

 Case study

Heather Fyfe, a Year 6 teacher and Year 5 and 6 team leader at Brixworth Primary School provides examples of how she sets targets for a pupil with dyslexia, then provides support for the pupil to meet the targets:

> When setting targets for a pupil I always make sure they are SMART – specific, measurable, achievable, realistic and set within a manageable time-frame. I set spelling targets by breaking down the unknown word list into groups of five. Each word is put onto a flashcard, which the pupil takes home and we also keep a set in school, so access to the words and practise of them is ongoing. After a week, the pupil is tested then another five words are added. At the end of a six-week half term the pupil will have learnt thirty spellings and they are encouraged to use them in their written work.

> To target writing, I use 'Tell me about it' cards. These are a series of situations put into picture form – for example, a family fishing trip is broken down into each step of the trip. Providing the pupil with the context for writing means they can focus on structuring sentences with detail for each picture and can then put the pictures together to make a story. Initially, I would set a target of completing two sentences per picture over a two-week period and expect the pupil to achieve this 80 per cent of the time. Once the pupil has successfully met the target, the number of sentences or level of detail within them would be increased.

Once the support has been agreed, this needs to be recorded and shared with everyone involved in supporting the child in the form of an ISP. What this is called and what this looks like will differ from one school to another. In the past, many schools used individual education plans (IEPs). However, the Code of Practice makes no reference to IEPs as it is recognised that some schools have found alternative, and often more effective, ways to record provision, support and ongoing outcomes. Other examples of ISPs include:

- Pupil Passports – a personal statement that outlines pupils' ambitions, strengths, difficulties and ways they prefer to be supported. It is written from the pupil's perspective and takes a holistic approach.

- One-page profiles – similar to the Pupil Passport, a one-page profile typically includes appreciation of the pupil and details of what is important to them and how to support them. The profile is written from the pupil's perspective. All the information is provided on one page, with a photograph of the pupil, so it is easier to take in at a glance.

- Individual provision map – outlines the additional provision a pupil is receiving and details who will be involved in delivering the provision, when the provision will take place and how the impact of the provision will be monitored.

An overview of the intervention pupils with SEN are receiving may also be recorded on a whole school provision map. This tool shows all the provision made which is additional to, and different from, that which is offered through the school's curriculum. In some primary schools, provision maps are written by the teacher on a class-by-class basis. In other schools, the provision map may be an overview of additional provision for the whole school and may be managed by the SENCO or heads of department.

Ask the pupil

Involving the pupil directly in developing their ISP gives them ownership over their learning and encourages them to become more independent. Consider the different opportunities you can give a pupil with SEN to articulate their strengths, concerns, aspirations and views on their learning. If a pupil finds this tricky because of their communication, cognitive or language difficulties, they may require support. This could entail:

- Promoting a classroom atmosphere of encouragement and acceptance so the pupil and their peers understand that everyone has different strengths and difficulties.

- Teaching the pupil how to make choices as a life skill; for example, using visual clues, objects of reference, photographs and symbols to support choice-making and communication.

- Modelling the language the pupil will need to use to express their needs and preferences – for example, 'I find it helps me to learn when … I find it difficult to learn when …'

- Using video to pre-record the pupil talking about their aspirations, likes and dislikes or to show examples of them learning in class or socialising with others.

- Preparing them for meetings and other situations where they will be discussing their progress and future by talking them through the process or role-playing.

Briony, a Year 5 pupil who has learning difficulties, explains the value of being listened to:

> Before, my other teacher just made me sit with Jamilia so she could help me if I got stuck but Jamilia didn't really talk to me so it wasn't very good. My new teacher asked me, 'Who do you want to sit next to?' I said Jacob because he sometimes helps me when we're at homework

club. Jacob helps me really well without just telling me what to do and it's much better and I get more done in lessons.

 Try it!

Ask your pupils

Do you know what pupils with SEN think of the way you support them in class? If not, try asking them:

- What is going well for you?

- What are you concerned about?

- What helps you when you are in my lessons?

- Is there anything that I could do to help you further?

- What can we do next?

If you don't think the pupil is likely to give you an honest response because they may be shy or don't want to offend you, ask a TA to talk to them and feed back.

For pupils with EHC plans, the process of planning graduated provision should be the same as it is for pupils receiving SEN support, although the needs of these pupils are likely to be more complex and the approach to meeting these needs will be even more personalised. Support is likely to include strategies, resources or programmes involving other professionals, such as a specialist teacher, educational psychologist or speech therapist. Provision will need to be planned so it focuses on the outcomes written in the pupil's EHC plan.

Do

The Code of Practice makes it clear that it is the responsibility of class and subject teachers to implement the ISP on a day-to-day basis. This might seem quite challenging, but don't forget that the SENCO is there to help. In practice, implementing the support plan will mean:

- Delivering HQT to the pupil in every lesson.

- Implementing any adjustments, specific strategies or approaches to classroom teaching that have been identified in the ISP.

- Managing any additional staff who are supporting pupils with SEN in your lessons.

- Implementing any targeted interventions or specialist provision, where this requires the involvement of the teacher.

- Continually assessing the pupil's progress and making any necessary adjustments to planning and teaching as a result.

- Monitoring and gathering evidence of the pupil's progress towards their identified outcomes or targets.

- Communicating regularly with the pupil, their parents, the SENCO and any other staff involved in order to establish how things are going and whether any changes are required.

Some pupils will be involved in interventions to develop the core curriculum areas of literacy or numeracy, or to improve other key skills such as communication, social and emotional skills or motor skills. As a class teacher, there may be times when you are directly involved in planning or managing the delivery of an intervention (particularly in primary). You will need to ensure you have a means of assessing the progress the pupil is making as a result of the additional provision. This will involve carrying out a baseline assessment at the start and comparing this with a follow-up assessment done at the end of the intervention. Some interventions come with their own assessment tools, but for others a suitable way of measuring impact will need to be developed. For example, if the intervention focuses on the development of reading skills, an assessment that measures reading age might be used. Evaluations of interventions should also take into account how well any individual targets have been achieved and how well the pupil is applying their learning in class.

If one of your pupils is involved in an intervention, make sure you know what the purpose of it is, what key skills are being taught and how you can support the pupil to transfer these skills in class. Often, a TA will be involved in delivering the intervention, so this will mean ensuring you get a chance to talk to them about it. If a TA is involved in intervention delivery, it is crucial they are provided with support in planning and delivering the programme, assessing the pupil's progress and reporting the outcomes. Further information on this is provided in Chapter 4.

 Did you know?

There are a large number of commercially produced interventions available for developing pupils' literacy and numeracy skills. The EEF have evaluated some of the available interventions. Take a look at: https://educationendowmentfoundation.org.uk/evaluation/projects/.

Review

The Code of Practice recommends that schools should review a pupil's ISP with parents at least three times each year. You will, of course, be continually reviewing pupil progress as part of your everyday classroom practice and as part of the whole school monitoring and review process. However, the SEN reviews will provide an opportunity to focus on the specifics of the support plan and to formally evaluate how successfully the support is meeting the needs of the pupil.

In some schools the SEN reviews may be incorporated as part of existing parents' meetings or progress days. In others, they may be arranged as additional, dedicated meetings. The review should be led by a teacher (or other member of staff) who knows the pupil well. In primary schools, this is likely to be their class teacher. In secondary, this may be their form tutor or key worker, the SENCO, another member of the SEN team or another identified lead professional. Therefore, depending on your role, you may or may not be directly involved in the review meeting. Even if you are not expected to lead or attend the meeting, you should still be contributing to the review process. This means keeping evidence of how well the pupil is progressing within your class and how effectively the additional support strategies are working.

When the review meeting between the pupil, parents and any relevant professionals takes place, it is helpful to consider the following questions:

- What progress has the pupil made? Has the pupil achieved their agreed targets and what is the evidence for this?

- What impact has the support/intervention had on progress?

- What are the pupil's and parents' views on the support/intervention?

- What are the teachers' and other professionals' views on the support/intervention?

- What changes need to be made to targets/support/intervention for next term?

- Do staff need any further training to secure greater success of the strategies or interventions?

The pupil's own views are very important to the review, and can be gathered either as part of the review meeting itself or beforehand, as part of the preparation for the meeting. If pupil voice is demonstrably valued and gathering pupils' views of their own learning is an intrinsic part of the teaching and learning process throughout the whole school, pupils will feel more comfortable in expressing their thoughts. At The Wroxham School in Hertfordshire, for example, all Year 5 and 6 pupils develop their own learner reviews twice a year. These are then used as the vehicle for the pupil, their family and the teaching team to discuss progress starting with, and from, the perspective of the child.

A record of the outcomes of the review discussions should be kept and used to update the pupil's ISP and any provision maps. The updated plan should then be shared with you and any other staff involved in supporting the pupil. You can use this to refine or adapt your own classroom practice.

Case study

Fez Pritish, a Year 7 form tutor from Manchester, explains how he supports the assess, plan, do, review cycle:

> In our school all form tutors in KS3 and KS4 are keyworkers for two or three pupils with SEN. We are responsible for ensuring Pupil Passports are completed. I do this by meeting with the pupil and their parents in October, once the pupil has had a chance to settle into school. We discuss what things the pupil feels helps them to learn and what things they struggle with. Next we identify two or three key non-curriculum targets for the pupil – these are often aimed at helping the pupil to organise themselves, improve their learning skills or help them develop socially. We identify four or five strategies the teachers should be using and things the pupil can do to help themselves, along with any support parents can provide at home.
>
> The Pupil Passports are put onto the network for all the pupil's teachers to access and they can come and talk to me or the SENCO if they want any help implementing the strategies on the plan.
>
> We try to review the Pupil Passports in February and June. A simple review form is emailed to all the pupil's teachers, which asks them to indicate where they think targets have been met and to note any particular successes or areas of concern. Although it's not always easy to meet face-to-face with parents at every review, the discussions we have when they do come in are so valuable – the process is much more than filling in a piece of paper!

The assess, plan, do, review process is a cycle: the idea being that this process is continual. If the review shows a pupil has made really good progress, this may mean they no longer require the additional provision made through SEN support. If this is the case, the pupil is likely to be taken off the SEN register or record and, instead, will be monitored to ensure progress is sustained through inclusive HQT. For others, the assess, plan, do, review cycle will continue and targets, strategies and provision will be revisited and refined. In successive cycles, the process becomes increasingly personalised, as everyone develops a growing understanding of the pupil's barriers to learning and the strategies needed to enable them to make progress. The graduated approach will only be effective, however, if you have high expectations and aspirations.

Just because a child has been identified as having SEN, this should not be an excuse for a lack of expected progress or lowered expectations!

Reflect

1. How do you make the best use of assessment information to identify pupils who are not making progress in your subject or in core areas of the curriculum?

2. How do you gather the views of pupils with SEN in your class? Is there anything else you can do to ensure they have the opportunity to express their views about their learning and progress?

3. How clear are you about your role in each of the stages of the assess, plan, do, review cycle? If there is something you would like clarifying, can you talk to your SENCO about it?

Further resources

SEN Support and the Graduated Approach, **nasen:** http://www.nasen.org.uk/resources/resources.sen-support-and-the-graduated-approach.html.
A brief guide which introduces school staff to the graduated approach to SEN support and outlines the role of class and subject teachers.

Individual support plan examples: http://www.nataliepacker.co.uk/#/resources/4551983811.
Visit my website for examples of ISPs and provision map templates.

Involving pupils in the planning process, Helen Sanderson Associates: http://www.helensandersonassociates.co.uk/person-centred-practice/person-centred-thinking-tools/.
This website provides examples of tools that can help to structure conversations and record pupils' responses when involving them in planning and reviewing support and provision.

Chapter 4

Working in partnership

If you teach a pupil who has complex needs, it's likely that there will be a range of additional people involved in supporting them. The pupil may be receiving help from TAs or other members of school staff. Perhaps they are also getting support from an educational psychologist, specialist teacher or speech therapist? Maybe they have health needs and a general practitioner or physiotherapist is also providing advice? Communicating regularly with those involved with the child will be key to ensuring a joined-up approach to meeting their needs – and central to this partnership will be the child's parents or carers.

Partnership with parents

As teachers, we understand what pupils are like when they are in our class, but parents have vital and unique knowledge about their child's needs and can bring a different perspective. Research by Henderson and Mapp suggests that when parents or carers are fully engaged in their children's learning, their children are more likely to attend school regularly, have better social skills and achieve better outcomes.[1] The Code of Practice recognises that parental involvement is particularly important for children and young people with additional needs, acknowledging that parents and carers know their child best of all. Parents should be fully involved in every step of the SEN process, from initial identification right through to making decisions about provision for their child with an EHC plan.

Developing positive relationships with parents starts at a whole school level. Initially, this involves establishing clear communication systems

---

1   See Anne T. Henderson and Karen L. Mapp, *A New Wave of Evidence The Impact of School, Family, and Community Connections on Student Achievement* (Austin, TX: Southwest Educational Development Laboratory and National Center for Family and Community Connections with Schools, 2002). Available at: https://www.sedl.org/connections/resources/evidence.pdf.

between parents and staff – for example, phone calls, texts or home–school liaison books – and setting up regular opportunities for meeting with parents: for example, parent forums, progress review meetings or coffee mornings. The school can then seek the views of parents on what's working well, or not so well, in terms of SEN provision, and act upon any feedback they receive.

? Did you know?

The Code of Practice advocates using person-centred approaches when planning for pupils with SEN. Person-centred planning is when a facilitator, such as a teacher or SENCO, works with a pupil and their parents, wider family, friends and professionals to gather information about the child: what their strengths are, what really matters to them and what the best ways of supporting them are. Parents are key partners in the process. The planning results in actions that are focused on the child or young person's learning and life and reflect their long-term aspirations.

The role of the teacher in working with parents

Working with the parents of children with SEN can be extremely beneficial. However, it can also be very challenging. You will come across families with a diverse range of needs and, for many parents, the issue of their child's SEN will be sensitive and emotionally charged. This can be especially true when a child is first diagnosed: being told their child has special needs is a difficult time for any parent and they will need time to come to terms with the diagnosis. Parents may hold different views to you and, although everyone wants the very best for the child, ideas as to what this might be and how to achieve it may vary! The key is to develop a positive relationship with parents so they can have professional trust in you and you can establish effective communication.

Listening to parents' concerns and hearing their point of view will go a long way to building that relationship. Anna, mum of Elijah who has autism, says:

> The most helpful thing the teacher can do is take the time to listen to me, take my concerns seriously and just let me know what's going well and what's not going so well with Elijah.

Simply giving parents the opportunity to talk about what their child is like at home and to share any concerns they have can provide a really useful insight into their child's strengths, interests and needs. It can also help you to empathise with the family and put yourself in their shoes, as far as this is possible. How would you feel if it was your child? What support would you want for them? What would you change to make things better? To promote positive relationships with parents:

- Make time for important conversations. Show you are *really* listening by making eye contact, summarising what has been said and keeping the focus on the child.

- Try to deal with any concerns on the day they arise. If you receive a phone call, try to return it as soon as possible, or ask someone else to ring on your behalf and let the parents know when you will be in touch.

- Be wary of using educational jargon or acronyms that parents may not understand (there are so many acronyms in SEN!).

- Avoid using negative language as it immediately creates hostility.

- When you are meeting parents as part of a review, check you have all the relevant information to hand – for example, the ISP, assessment information, pupil's views and reports from specialists.

- Keep a record of any important discussions you have with parents, particularly if there is likely to be a follow up afterwards or potential issues may arise as a result of the conversation.

- Recognise the realities of life for some parents of children with SEN (lack of sleep and high stress levels, for example) and consider the practical implications of when meetings are held, to avoid childcare issues. Recognising and acknowledging how parents are feeling can immediately give comfort and reassurance and often de-escalates a difficult situation.

■ Make sure communication happens for positive reasons too. If the pupil has done something really well, let the parents know!

 Try it!

Parent postcards

Although most schools use texts or emails to communicate with parents, using good old-fashioned postcards to share positive comments means the pupil can physically present the card to their parents (and the parents can even display the postcard on the fridge door!). Alternatively, try investing in a talking postcard. These contain a voice-recording chip so you, or the pupil, can record a brief verbal message for the parent, and the parent can choose to record a message in return. Talking postcards can provide a great opportunity for pupils with speech and language difficulties to practise their speaking skills by recording their own message.

No matter how hard you try, you won't always agree with parents and you won't always be able to help them with their concerns or allay their fears. When you're talking to parents about their child, at times they may become upset or angry – don't take it personally as it's usually the situation they are expressing negative feelings towards rather than you. Getting others, such as the SENCO, on board can be helpful, particularly if you are worried about meeting with parents and know there may be difficult conversations brewing!

Effective partnerships with TAs

 Did you know?

There are currently more TAs in schools than ever before. In fact, more than 25 per cent of the UK school workforce consists of TAs.[2]

When you have a TA or other adult in a lesson, what do you ask them to do? What do you see as their responsibility? TAs can fulfil a range of roles and duties, however, they are often tasked with supporting pupils with SEN or those deemed to be 'lower ability'. But is this always the most effective way to deploy them? Although many teachers think that providing additional adult support will help a pupil to achieve better, research carried out by the Institute of Education (IOE) in 2009 showed that the pupils who had the most support from TAs made the least progress![3] This was mainly due to the fact that the pupils were getting most of their 'teaching' input from the TA rather than the teacher. In addition, TAs were often doing too much for the pupils and this was leading to 'learned helplessness', an unintended consequence of *too much* support, where the pupil cannot cope without adult input and lacks the skills to tackle learning independently.

The research from the IOE demonstrates that teachers and senior leaders need to have a clear, well-thought-out strategy about the most effective way of deploying TAs. Could the TA in your class, for example, work with a different group or oversee the rest of the class while you focus on the pupils with additional needs? If the TA is working with a pupil with SEN, do they encourage the pupil to be independent by providing initial

---

2   Department for Education, *School Workforce in England: November 2015* (2016). Ref: SFR 21/2016. Available at: https://www.gov.uk/government/statistics/school-workforce-in-england-november-2015, p. 4.

3   Peter Blatchford, Paul Bassett, Penelope Brown, Clare Martin, Anthony Russell and Rob Webster, *The Deployment and Impact of Support Staff Project*. Research Brief: DCSF-RB148 (London: DCSF, 2009). Available at: http://maximisingtas.co.uk/assets/content/dissressum.pdf.

input then moving away from them? How are they supporting a range of pupils in your class to make progress?

As with parents, the key to building a good partnership with TAs is effective communication. Initially, this means setting clear boundaries and expectations around roles, behaviour management and strategies the TA will be using. Establishing agreement regarding classroom structures and routines will provide a solid foundation for your professional working relationship to develop.

 Case study

At St James' Catholic High School in Barnet, TAs and teachers work in close partnership and teachers ensure that TAs support the whole class, not just a few individuals. One way this has been achieved is through the introduction of the Teacher–Teaching Assistant Agreement. A few weeks into the start of the new academic year, teachers sit down with TAs to discuss expectations of their working partnership. This includes a list of roles for the TA to perform during different parts of the lesson (e.g. during the introduction, group work, etc.) and agreements around behaviour management. There are also examples of specific strategies for TAs to use with individual students, focusing on those requiring additional support.

Geography teacher Alex Aldridge says the agreements have had a real impact on teaching and learning, as the discussion allows a two-way sharing of ideas and is especially useful when teachers are working with more than one TA. In his class, the TA will often write down keywords on the board while he is talking, join in with asking and answering questions and provide support for recording and understanding homework. Alex says, 'The relationship between the TA and the teacher is crucial, it really helps to move the lesson forward.'

If you have TA support during a lesson, you will need to carefully plan how they will be deployed effectively. Many excellent schools provide time and resources to allow their TAs to plan with teachers. However, this isn't always possible, in which case it is still important that you consider the best way to share your planning with the TA before the start of the lesson. Provide them with a copy of the lesson plan or notes and check they understand what you want them to do. Even if you can only manage a two-minute conversation just prior to the lesson, it's better than nothing! The TA needs to be clear about the overall learning objectives and success criteria for the lesson, what their role will be and any specific strategies you would like them to use. Also confirm how you expect them to assess progress, record outcomes and feed back to you.

Teachers can sometimes be criticised for not making the best use of TAs when they are providing whole class input. Make sure this doesn't happen in your class by asking the TA to do some of the following:

- Model expected learning behaviours or support pupils to keep focused.

- Model the task or the use of specific equipment while you are explaining it.

- Reword instructions or questions for pupils who find language difficult.

- Write observational notes to support assessment – e.g. on pupils' contributions to discussions.

- Support pupils to access the lesson/materials – e.g. modifying resources.

- Pre-teach pupils who need additional support – e.g. with subject-specific vocabulary or to start them off on the task.

During the main part of the lesson, the TA may be working with identified individuals or groups, or the majority of the class. Whichever pupils they are working with, their role is to help move the learning forward and support pupils to learn independently through the use of a variety of pedagogical techniques. This might involve them:

- reinforcing key concepts/skills/vocabulary

- re-modelling or re-explaining

- scribing for the teacher on the board or scribing for a pupil

- reinforcing instructions and checking understanding

- helping pupils to use practical equipment or resources

- encouraging discussion and participation

- questioning pupils to challenge them in their learning

- assessing pupils' learning through observation, questioning and discussion, and checking and clarifying misconceptions

- helping to make links between learning in the lesson and other contexts

- supporting pupils to identify their next steps in learning and what they need to do to achieve them

If a pupil has an EHC plan, the arrangements for additional educational provision may include time during the day when the pupil is given one-to-one support from an adult. If a TA is working one-to-one with a pupil, they are likely to be most effective when they are scaffolding the pupil's learning by monitoring the progress they are making towards the learning objectives or goals, providing immediate feedback and giving targeted support with parts of the task the pupil finds difficult (revisit further examples of scaffolding by looking back at page 44 in Chapter 2). Remember that, even when a TA is working one-to-one with a pupil, it remains your responsibility as the teacher to plan for the pupil – you are responsible for their overall progress.

Try it!

Developing TAs' questioning skills

Encourage TAs to develop their pedagogical skills by allowing them to spend a lesson observing the questioning techniques you use. After the lesson, discuss the observation together and agree ways in which the TA could use similar techniques with groups or individuals. Share the questioning matrix in the EEF's guidance report, which can support TAs to structure open and closed questions.[4]

Agree on the ways you will gather feedback from your TA. Have a brief chat with them at the end of the lesson or, if time doesn't allow for this, ask them to make comments on sticky notes that can be left on your desk before they leave. If the TA has been working with an individual or group, provide them with a simple feedback form to record how well pupils met the learning objectives, anything they struggled with and any suggestions for next steps. This information will help you with your planning for the following lesson.

Interventions

TAs may sometimes be involved in delivering targeted intervention programmes designed to consolidate pupils' key skills, perhaps in literacy, numeracy or social development. The intervention might take place within the classroom or elsewhere, in small groups, pairs or one-to-one. More often than not, the intervention will be structured and advice on how to deliver it will be built in. However, the TA may still require

---

4   Jonathan Sharples, Rob Webster and Peter Blatchford, *Making Best Use of Teaching Assistants: Guidance Report* (London: Education Endowment Foundation, 2015). Available at: https://educationendowmentfoundation.org.uk/uploads/pdf/TA_Guidance_Report_Interactive.pdf.

additional guidance. Ensure there are opportunities for the TA to do the following:

■ Develop a sound understanding of the purpose of the intervention.

■ Look through the content, plan how they will deliver it and sort out necessary resources.

■ Get to know the profiles of the pupils they are working with.

■ Develop a sound understanding of the pedagogical skills they will need to use to deliver the intervention effectively – for example, modelling, questioning, feedback.

■ Understand how they will assess the pupils involved, both at the start of the intervention and again at the end to show progress.

■ Monitor and review the progress pupils are making throughout the intervention.

■ Understand how to feed back the outcomes to the teacher or SENCO.

If you are managing an intervention, you will need to support the TA to ensure they are confident they can deliver it effectively. If you're not directly involved, it is still important to discuss the key skills the pupils are focusing on with the TA and agree how you can both support the pupils to transfer what they have learned back into the classroom.

 Case study

A TA at St Mary's Primary School in Barnet describes her role:

> I support one particular pupil with her speech and language development by delivering scheduled sessions and encouraging her to apply the same strategies in the classroom. Knowing what resources and particular approaches are effective for her is crucial. Paired writing, frequent reading, simple instructions and visual aids assist her learning and enable her to take responsibility for her own learning. The most important part of my role is to support each pupil with SEN in a way that helps them to become independent.

> Assessing this particular pupil is a continual process. This is done both in a formal way through the use of tests and informally on an ongoing basis. Knowing the individual pupil well, and understanding her needs, allows me to contribute effectively to the teacher's weekly plans. I suggest ways to adapt lessons to suit the child based on any concerns I may have.
>
> I contribute to her Pupil Passport and refer to it regularly. Together with the pupil, her teacher and I look at her targets and review progress. I always have high expectations and encourage her to work to her full potential. Integral to all of this is working in partnership and communicating effectively with the teacher.

There are many incredibly skilled and talented TAs in our schools who show initiative, creativity and, very importantly, lots of patience! They can add enormous value to what happens in the classroom, enabling pupils to engage in lessons and make progress. However, this will only happen if you communicate effectively and you work together as a team. Remember that, ultimately, it is *your* responsibility as the teacher to direct them and ensure they are making a difference to pupils' learning.

The role of the SENCO

Throughout this book the focus has been on the increased responsibility of the class or subject teacher in meeting the needs of pupils with SEN. Just as the role of the teacher has changed over the last few years, so has the role of the SENCO. In order to be really effective, their role needs to be a much more strategic one, working with the head teacher and governors to determine the direction of SEN policy and coordinate provision across the school. They oversee the day-to-day operation of the school's SEN policy, advise on the graduated approach to providing SEN support and ensure that the school keeps the records of all pupils with SEN up to date. They also liaise with parents of pupils with SEN and are a key point of contact for other SEN professionals, such as educational psychologists and speech therapists.

? **Did you know?**

The role of the SENCO is a vital one. It is a statutory requirement for all maintained schools, academies and free schools to have a qualified SENCO.

An increasingly important aspect of the SENCO's role is providing professional guidance to colleagues. Your SENCO should be able to provide you with advice to ensure you can effectively meet your responsibilities towards pupils with SEN. So, in what ways might they support you? The SENCO could:

- Help you identify pupils' strengths and needs and understand any potential barriers to their learning.

- Support you with curriculum planning for pupils with SEN.

- Provide advice on strategies to use in the classroom as part of HQT for pupils with SEN or model strategies while you observe.

- Help you to set appropriately challenging targets for individual pupils with SEN or develop their ISPs.

- Join you in meetings with parents or other professionals.

- Give guidance on deploying TAs in your classroom.

- Suggest ideas for implementing additional interventions within the classroom.

- Provide mentoring or coaching to support you in identifying areas for development around SEN.

As well as the SENCO, there will be other colleagues who can support you and with whom you can work collaboratively. There are real benefits to problem solving with others, sharing strategies and ideas to try in the classroom, jointly planning lessons or observing others teaching.

Try it!

Sharing practice

Sit down with a colleague and take a look at the HQT jigsaw on page 30 of Chapter 2. Identify an aspect of HQT for pupils with SEN that you would both like to develop. Share practical ideas for implementing this in your classroom and agree on one or two actions to both try over the next week or so. Arrange to meet again to reflect on the outcomes.

Working with other SEN professionals

The Code of Practice makes it clear that if children and young people with SEN are to achieve the best possible outcomes, then education, health and social care services must work together to ensure they get the right support. Some individuals, particularly those with complex needs, may require input from all three services so a joined-up approach, which puts the individual and their family at the centre, is crucial.

A wide range of professionals might work with the individuals you teach. Specialist support services, for example, can advise on teaching techniques and strategies, classroom management, curriculum development and use of resources. Some LAs have specialist teachers who provide support for particular areas of need, such as VI or SpLD. An educational psychologist will carry out more specialised assessments and suggest further strategies to try with the pupil. They also offer advice on staff development as part of a whole school approach. Many younger children may have input from a speech and language therapist to support delayed speech or language and communication development.

Health professionals are able to offer advice on managing a wide range of conditions. Physiotherapists will provide support for those with PD while clinical psychologists will work with children and young people who have mental health issues or poor emotional well-being. Some families may also be receiving support from social services, perhaps to help with a family problem, as a result of child protection issues or because the child has been placed in foster care. Private specialists or organisations can also offer expertise in specific areas – for example, autism or VI. Pages 167–168 provide a list of some of the professionals you are most likely to come across.

If one of your pupils is having a visit in school time from another professional, make sure you understand:

- What their role is.

- Why they are coming and what they will be doing.

- When they will be visiting and if the pupil will be expected to leave your lesson to meet with them.

- If and when you will have the opportunity to communicate with them, either during or after their visit.

Don't be afraid to ask the professional questions so you can gain a better understanding of their role and how to help the pupil, although do bear in mind that some professionals' input will be confidential, so sharing of information will be limited. If one of your pupils has recently received advice or assessment, check that you have been given any information that is relevant to you. External agency reports can be quite technical and can include language that won't necessarily be familiar to teachers. If there is anything that you don't understand or would like clarifying, don't forget that your SENCO is there to help: a team approach to supporting the child usually works best.

 Case study

Bruce Waelend, education consultant and former head teacher of St James' Primary School in Emsworth, reflects on the importance of everyone working together to support pupils with SEN:

> While it's certainly the responsibility of the class teacher to ensure their pupils with SEN make progress, they would not be able to succeed without the help of an excellent SENCO, TAs, leaders and

other professionals firmly behind them. Nor would they flourish if teachers before them had not done their job. An exceptional SENCO, for example, acts as a source of expertise, contacts and ideas to support the teacher. I think of those heroic people who choose to undertake brave and daring deeds such as swimming the channel. While there's only one name on the certificate or news headline, it's always a team effort. There's always someone in the boat telling the swimmer how they're doing, encouraging them and making sure that they have everything they need. It's the same with teaching. While the teacher is the one who has to ultimately do the job, it's also a team effort and without that team no class teacher would be able to achieve the very best for pupils – whether they have SEN or not.

 Reflect

1. How effectively do you develop relationships with parents of pupils with SEN? Is there anything that works particularly well? Is there anything you could do to improve the relationships further?

2. What evidence do you have that TAs make a difference to pupils' learning in your class? Is there anything else you could do to support them in their role?

3. Consider a pupil who receives support from other professionals. Do you know what these professionals do and how they support the pupil? Is there any additional information you would like to find out from them or the SENCO?

 **Further resources**

***Working in Partnership with Parents and Carers,* nasen:** http://www.nasen.org.uk/resources/resources.working-in-partnership-with-parents-and-carers.html.

A quick guide outlining how schools can work closely with parents and carers to meet the needs of pupils with SEN.

***Making Best Use of Teaching Assistants,* Jonathan Sharples, Rob Webster and Peter Blatchford:** https://educationendowmentfoundation.org.uk/uploads/pdf/TA_Guidance_Report_Interactive.pdf.

A guidance report containing seven recommendations to maximise the impact of TAs in primary and secondary schools, based on the best available research evidence.

The Teaching Assistant's Guide to Effective Interaction: *How to Maximise Your Practice*, **Paula Bosanquet, Julie Radford and Rob Wester**

Practical ideas for TAs and teachers managing TAs based on the IOE research around effective deployment of additional adults.

Working with Outside Agencies: A Framework for Consultation – Class Teacher, nasen: http://www.sendgateway.org.uk/resources.working-with-outside-agencies-a-framework-for-consultation-class-teacher.html.

A best practice video from nasen showing how a primary teacher works with an educational psychologist to support a pupil in her class.

Part 2

The teacher's toolkit

Introducing the areas of need

Imagine the following scenario: in your class of thirty you have four pupils who have SEN. One has MLD, one has autism and another has PD. The fourth pupil has been diagnosed with dyslexia and also has traits of dyspraxia and possibly ADD. You are a brilliant, inclusive teacher and have all the elements of HQT in place. But what else can you do to meet the very specific needs of these pupils requiring SEN support as part of the graduated approach?

Part 2 of this book aims to help you to meet the needs of pupils with particular difficulties. It provides information on certain types of SEN which will be particularly useful at the initial 'assess' stage of the SEN support cycle (assess, plan, do, review). This section also gives you a toolkit of strategies to try. These will support the 'plan' and 'do' stages of the cycle. The section is divided into the four broad areas of need outlined in the Code of Practice. These four areas are intended to give an overview of the range of needs that schools should be planning for. Within each of the broad areas, a number of different difficulties can be identified. This section of the book aims to provide information and guidance on selected difficulties: it is by no means exhaustive, but it does focus on some of the more common areas of need that you are likely to come across as a mainstream teacher.

The types of SEN covered within each broad area are as follows:

Chapter 5: Communication and interaction

■ Speech, language and communication needs (SLCN)

■ Autistic spectrum disorder (ASD)

Chapter 6: Cognition and learning

■ Moderate learning difficulties (MLD)

■ Specific learning difficulties (SpLD): dyslexia, dyscalculia, dyspraxia

Chapter 7: Social, emotional and mental health difficulties

- Mental health

- Attention deficit hyperactivity disorder (ADHD)

Chapter 8: Sensory and/or physical needs

- Visual impairment (VI)

- Hearing impairment (HI)

- Physical disability (PD)

For each area of need, some of the more common characteristics and associated behaviours a pupil *may* display are highlighted, as are some of the difficulties they *may* face. The list is not necessarily comprehensive, neither is it intended to be diagnostic; it simply provides an outline of characteristics which *may* be apparent compared to the majority of same-age peers. Similarly, it is not the intention to encourage a deficit model of SEN, as adopting this view can limit what we believe a pupil is capable of achieving. The purpose of highlighting potential barriers to learning is in order to use this information as a starting point to gain a good understanding of each child in order to develop their individual capacity to learn. This information will be particularly useful at the initial 'assess' stage of the SEN support cycle (assess, plan, do, review).

Each section also gives a description of some of the strategies you *may* find useful in supporting a pupil with a particular need. These strategies aim to support the 'plan' and 'do' stages of the graduated approach cycle: however, they are not intended to be read as a must-do list. Remember that each child is unique; we must ensure they are respected as individuals and not defined by a label. The profile of one child with autism, for example, will be very different to the profile of another child with autism. Be open-minded about what might work best and use your professional judgement to consider what is right for an individual pupil. Knowing the pupil well (yes, we're back to this again!), building on their strengths and understanding why certain strategies *might* be useful for them is the starting point for making decisions about what SEN support will look like in your classroom.

Chapter 5

Communication and interaction

Speech, language and communication needs (SLCN)

SLCN is an umbrella term used to describe those children or young people who have difficulty communicating with others. This may be because they find it challenging to say what they want to, they have difficulty understanding what is being said to them or they do not understand social rules of communication.

There are many different types of SLCN, including:

- Speech and language delay – speech and language development isn't what would be expected for a child of that age.

- Receptive language difficulty – problems with understanding words, sentences or instructions.

- Expressive language difficulty – issues with using language to express ideas, needs or feelings.

- Speech or articulation difficulty – a difficulty saying words clearly using the correct sounds.

- Social interaction difficulty – problems following the rules of communication and difficulty interacting socially with others.

SLCN is the most common type of SEN in primary schools. However, The Communication Trust suggests there are many more children, in both primary and secondary schools, who have difficulties in this area that go unidentified.[1]

---

1 See The Communication Trust, *A Generation Adrift: The Case for Speech, Language and Communication to Take a Central Role in Schools' Policy and Practice* (London: The Communication Trust, 2013), p. 14.

? Did you know?

Two-thirds of 7 to 14-year-olds with serious behaviour problems have language impairment. Over half of all children who have persistent language difficulties go on to have problems with reading.[2]

The profile for each child with SLCN will be very different. However, a pupil may have difficulties with some or all of the following:

- Forming letters, speech sounds or words.

- Blending or segmenting words when talking.

- Finding the right word or joining words together to make sense.

- Using or understanding key vocabulary.

- Making conversation with peers or joining in play that involves language.

- Understanding jokes or more complex language such as idioms.

- Joining in class discussions.

- Following instructions or understanding what has just been said to them.

- Staying on topic when talking and making themself understood.

Sometimes children and young people with SLCN can misunderstand other people's actions or intentions or their communication can come across as insulting or rude when they don't mean it to be. Often, pupils can become self-conscious of or frustrated by their inability to communicate with others. This can lead to behavioural difficulties or negative social relationships, pupils may become angry at their peers or choose to withdraw from activities that involve communication. In secondary school, young people with SLCN can be particularly vulnerable to

---

2   See https://www.thecommunicationtrust.org.uk/media/2612/communication_
    difficulties_-_facts_and_stats.pdf.

teasing or bullying from peers. Josh, a Year 8 pupil with expressive language difficulties, recently told his form tutor:

> Others in my class have to listen harder and make more effort to understand what I'm saying to them so some of them just don't bother talking to me in the first place.

Classroom strategies

As part of the 'assess' stage of the SEN support cycle, start by finding out about the profile of the pupil. Is their speech delayed? Do they have a receptive or expressive language difficulty? Do they find social communication a challenge? Gathering further information will help you to decide which of the following strategies will be worth trying:

- Set up a 'communication-friendly' classroom, aiming to make communication as easy, effective and enjoyable as possible where:

  - The space and layout enable different opportunities for talking.

  - Noise levels are such that everyone can hear and be heard.

  - There are clear and consistent routines around communication – e.g. for turn-taking when speaking.

  - Visual aids are used to support language development – e.g. easy-to-understand signs, visual timetables using symbols, photographs.

- Provide good models of speech by speaking clearly and not too quickly. Sometimes it may be appropriate to use shorter sentences.

- Provide lots of opportunities for the pupil to talk. This might be through a learning activity such as role-play or by asking the pupil to take a short verbal message to another member of staff. Where there is paired talk, ensure the pupil is working with a peer who is a positive speaking and listening role model.

- Ask the pupil to repeat what you've said in their own words, so you will know how much they have understood. This is particularly useful when you have given instructions.

- Use props to encourage the pupil to talk more – e.g. a mobile phone or video camera. With younger pupils, try using a puppet; often children are less reluctant to talk to a puppet than a 'real' person because they feel less likely to be judged. For older children, using an avatar can work as an alternative to a puppet.

Learning new, subject-specific vocabulary can often be tricky for pupils with SLCN. Pre-tutoring them by introducing keywords before a lesson can help pupils feel more prepared and give them confidence in class. Provide lots of opportunities for them to review and revise keywords through fun activities, such as the one below.

 Try it!

What am I?

Have you ever played the party game where someone puts a sticky note with the name of a famous person written on it on your forehead? This game is similar, but instead of famous people, keywords related to the lesson topic are used. Pupils ask questions to try to discover what the word on their forehead is.

For a pupil who has difficulties with expression or sound articulation, allow time for them to formulate a response when speaking. Try not to jump in too soon or speak for them as this can undermine their efforts and lead them to thinking there's no point in even trying to speak. Although the pupil is likely to be sensitive to others' potential difficulties in understanding them, don't pretend to understand what they say to you if you really don't! If the pupil makes errors in their speech, rather than correcting them, model the right use of spoken language. Younger pupils in particular will benefit from opportunities to develop phonological awareness by playing games involving alliteration, rhyme, syllables, blending and segmenting. Take a look at The Communication Trust's guide *Communicating Phonics* for further ideas.[3]

---

3   See https://www.thecommunicationtrust.org.uk/resources/resources/resources-for-practitioners/communicating-phonics/.

Try it!

Trampoline

Try this activity as a fun way for pupils to practise listening and distinguishing sounds. Pupils sit on the floor or on their chairs – they will need enough space around them to stand up and sit down again. Tell the pupils you are going to read a short piece of text and they must listen out for words beginning with a particular sound, e.g. 'th'. Choose a text that has a good number of examples of the identified sound and read out a few paragraphs or pages. The first time the pupils hear the identified sound they must stand up, the next time they hear it they sit down and so on.

For a pupil who struggles with the social use of language, try the following:

- Praise the pupil when they use good listening skills and be explicit about what they are doing well – e.g. 'I can see you are listening to what I'm saying because you're looking at me and nodding.'

- Devise class rules about who can speak and when during whole class or group discussions. Do you always expect hands up to ask or answer a question? Should only one person speak at a time?

- Try to explain the effect it has on the other person if the pupil breaks social communication rules – e.g. 'If you talk when someone else is talking, they will think you don't want to hear what they have to say and that will make them feel sad or frustrated.' This can be explored further through role-play or games.

- Encourage the pupil to look at non-verbal cues to help them understand what the other person thinks and feels – e.g. 'If someone is turning their head away from you all the time when you are talking, they might not be listening to what you are saying.'

■ Explicitly teach the pupil useful phrases for conversation – e.g. 'Can I just say …?' or 'Sorry to interrupt, but …'

Try it!

Barrier games

Barrier games are activities in which two people are working to achieve the same result without being able to see each other. They are an excellent way of practising a range of communication skills, including active listening, following instructions and using specific vocabulary. To play a barrier game, you'll need the following:

■ Two players: a listener and a speaker (this could be two pupils or a pupil and an adult).

■ Two sets of the same materials – e.g. small building blocks, miniature objects, play dough, picture cards, drawing materials.

■ A barrier (for example a screen or a large book that will stand up) placed in between the two players so they cannot see each other's materials. This means that there are no longer any visual clues available within the game and the success of the activity relies on good verbal communication.

The speaker arranges their materials and describes to the listener what they are doing – e.g. 'I am putting the small red block on top of the large blue block.' The aim of the game is for the listener to arrange their materials in the same way. When the listener has finished, the barrier is removed and the arrangement of the two sets of materials are compared. The game can also be played with the speaker describing a picture to the listener, who has to draw it.

Some children and young people with SLCN may benefit from speech and language therapy. This involves a specialist teacher or speech and language therapist working with the pupil to develop a personalised programme of support. The programme may be delivered by the specialist themselves or by someone else who has been trained, for example a TA.

Specialists can also offer support with the use of augmentative and alternative communication (AAC). This is the term used to describe various methods of communication that can support those who find speech a challenge. Examples include Makaton (a language programme using signs and symbols), Picture Exchange Communication System (PECS) (a communication system using pictures for those with complex needs) or voice output communication aids (VOCAs).

 Case study

Jemima, a Reception class teacher from Halifax, describes the strategies she uses to support one of her pupils who has speech and language difficulties:

> Jack is a lively 5-year-old who has difficulties understanding language, particularly complex sentences. He also has poor listening skills and finds it hard to articulate sounds.
>
> When the pupils are sat on the carpet, Jack sits right in front of me so I can focus his attention and give him support if he doesn't understand what is being said. When I give him instructions, I keep them very simple and I use gestures to prompt him. Jack likes animals and puppets so we use Arnold the dog to engage Jack in conversation and give him plenty of opportunities to practise speaking and listening.
>
> Jack has been receiving weekly sessions from a speech therapist and my TA has also been attending the sessions so she can learn the articulation exercises the therapist has been using. She spends ten minutes each day working on them with Jack. She uses a mirror to show Jack the position his mouth should be in when making sounds and she continually models how the sounds are made. They play lots of games associating sounds with an object, action, or noise to help practise sounds in a fun way.

Autistic spectrum disorder (ASD)

ASD is a complex lifelong developmental disorder that affects the way a person experiences the world around them, communicates and relates to others. ASD, also known as autistic spectrum condition (ASC), is thought of in terms of a continuum, ranging from mild to severe and can affect individuals in many different ways. Many young people with autism are not diagnosed until the age of 11 or older. Asperger syndrome is a form of autism. Children with Asperger syndrome are often of average or above average intelligence but may still have difficulties with understanding and processing language.

 Did you know?

Statistics vary, but boys are at least four times more likely than girls to be identified with ASD according to some studies.[4] However, it is believed that ASD is under-diagnosed in females, possibly because their behaviour can conflict with some of the more 'typical' core characteristics of ASD, such as the ability to form friendships.

Each child or young person with autism is unique. However, they do tend to have difficulties in three main areas. These have been referred to as the triad of impairments. These three areas are:

1. **Social interaction.** This includes problems with recognising and understanding the feelings of other people and with managing their own feelings. Pupils with ASD often lack the skills to interact with other people appropriately and this can make it difficult for them to form friendships. They can appear to be focused on themselves and may seem to have little or no understanding regarding what other people think or feel. Some pupils

---

4   For example Stephan Ehlers and Christopher Gillberg's research into Asperger syndrome, The Epidemiology of Asperger Syndrome, *Journal of Child Psychology and Psychiatry* (November 1993), 34 (8): 1327–1350. See http://www.autism.org.uk/about/what-is/gender.aspx.

can become highly distressed if someone encroaches on their personal space.

2. **Social communication**. This can include difficulties with using and understanding verbal and non-verbal language, such as gestures, eye contact, facial expressions and tone of voice. Pupils can fail to answer when they are spoken to directly. When they do communicate, they often talk about their own interests, rather than listening to others: they may have difficulty holding a two-way conversation. They may use limited, repetitive phrases or echo the speech of others. Inferring anything other than the literal meaning of spoken phrases is often challenging (for example, the expression 'it's raining cats and dogs' can be quite distressing for a child with autism!).

3. **Social imagination**. This includes the ability to understand and predict other people's intentions and behaviour or to imagine situations outside of their own experience. Difficulties in the area of imagination and thought lead to a lack of flexibility in thinking and behaviour. This makes it challenging for pupils to cope with new and unfamiliar situations. Some pupils prefer to engage in a narrow, repetitive range of activities, perhaps playing with objects in a ritualistic way, and will be resistant to change, preferring rigid adherence to routines and rituals.

According to the National Autistic Society, between 44 and 52 per cent of people with ASD may also have a learning disability.[5] They may demonstrate a delay in spoken language or find developing reading skills challenging. A pupil with ASD may also experience over- or under-sensitivity to sounds, touch, tastes, smells, light or colours. Some can be unaware of common dangers, such as fire, have difficulties with personal organisation or have dietary or medical issues such as problems with digestion or toileting. Despite their challenges, because of their different view of the world, people with ASD can show others a different perspective on everyday situations and be very engaging.

---

5   See http://www.autism.org.uk/about/what-is/myths-facts-stats.aspx.

Classroom strategies

Structure and routine

One of the most effective ways of supporting pupils with ASD is to create a well-structured environment to reduce unpredictability and allow the pupil to make sense of what's around them. Use very clear classroom routines that you consistently reinforce with the pupil (how to line up, how to ask for help from an adult, how to show they are listening to others, etc.).

■ Seat the pupil in an area of the classroom that is free from clutter and distractions, or provide a calm, distraction-free work area in the classroom where pupils can choose to work (see the example of the work station on page 36 in Chapter 2).

■ Allow the pupil to remove themselves to an agreed calm-down area if they become anxious or frustrated. Use a time-out card so the pupil can simply show the card to indicate they would like to move, or leave the room, without having to verbalise this to you.

■ A pupil with ASD is likely to benefit from the use of pictorial instructions and visual timetables. A visual timetable uses pictures, symbols or photographs to show each activity over the course of the day – e.g. registration, English, PE, lunchtime.

■ Give the pupil advance warning about any changes in routine. Explain to them the reasons for the changes and help them to prepare – e.g. by demonstrating on a visual timetable when the change will happen or talking through the new routine with them. If a pupil is struggling with unstructured times of the day, for example break time, provide them with a structured activity to do – e.g. playing a game with a peer, going to a club, reading a book.

Try it!

Finished!

When using visual timetables, once the activity is finished, remove the picture, photograph or symbol from the timetable and place in a 'finished' pouch to indicate it is time to move on to the next activity. For older pupils, encourage them to manage their own written timetable that they can cross out as each activity is completed.

Use of language

If a pupil finds using and understanding language difficult, try to keep it simple and consistent and, where appropriate, use repetition. A pupil with ASD can find it particularly confusing when the same word is used in different contexts and has a different meaning, for example, the words 'odd' and 'volume' have specific meanings when used in a mathematical context. Beware of using sarcasm as pupils with ASD may find this difficult to understand and avoid or explain metaphorical language and idioms such as 'in a minute' or 'pull your socks up'!

When you are giving instructions:

- Use the pupil's name to get their attention before speaking to them.

- Make eye contact easier by getting down to the pupil's level.

- Give them one or two at a time and ask the pupil to repeat each instruction back to check their understanding.

- Be very specific – e.g. 'I would like you to think of three questions to ask Sarah, your talk partner, about the book she has just finished reading.'

Try it!

Key ring instructions

Create small cards with simple instructions such as 'stop', 'no' and 'choose'. Display the cards on a key ring for the pupil or an adult to wear to refer to when needed. This will provide easily accessible visual support for a pupil with limited understanding of language.

Social interaction

■ Create opportunities for the pupil to interact with their peers through group work or shared activities. When a pupil with ASD is expected to work in a group, give clear roles to each group member. Remember to provide some opportunities for the pupil to also work alone, when appropriate.

■ Be aware that a pupil with ASD may need additional support with activities requiring them to use their imagination, express emotions or empathise. If the pupil is expected to write about feelings or use their imagination, provide them with scaffolds to enable them to do so – e.g. pictures to represent emotions or ideas for starting a story.

■ If the pupil becomes anxious, aggressive or distressed, stay calm (and try not to take it personally!). They are unlikely to understand their own feelings and emotions so will find it difficult to control them.

Try it!

Social story

This is a short story that describes exactly what happens in a particular social situation – for example, getting ready for school, going to lunch, getting changed for PE, joining in a group discussion. The story can be used as a script that the pupil can refer to as a way of helping them cope in situations that they might find challenging. For further information on social stories, go to: http://carolgraysocialstories.com.

Support for transition

Any changes in routine can be stressful for a child with ASD and they can be particularly vulnerable when moving class or transferring from one school to another. The move from primary to secondary school often means higher demands on personal organisation, as they will need to follow timetables and meet deadlines. They will need to use social skills as they get used to more adults and learn to cope with a change of peer group. As secondary schools tend to be bigger and busier environments, there can be a greater risk of sensory overload for the pupil. Martin, who has ASD and is now in Year 9, recalls his first term at secondary school:

> I was very anxious because the school was large and I couldn't find my way around. When we had to change lessons there was so much noise with all the other students milling around, going from one place to another. One day I had to hide in an empty classroom until the noise had stopped because it was too much for me.

The SENCO will play a key role in liaising with staff from the other school and with parents, and perhaps organising for the pupil to have extra visits to help them prepare and become familiar with the school. However, class teachers can also offer support by providing strategies to help them organise their personal belongings or read lesson timetables.

Encourage the pupil to develop their own pen portrait (in writing or through a video or blog) that can be shared with key members of staff at the new school to provide useful information about the pupil, from their own perspective.

 Case study

Cate Marsden, assistant head teacher at Ladywood School and Outreach Service in Bolton, outlines some of the strategies she uses to support a Year 1 pupil with ASD:

> The use of visuals to support all aspects of social and academic learning is so important. Visuals help a child with ASD remember, and make sense of, the structure and expectations of the day. I use visual timetables, visual schedules, task baskets and tick lists to help the pupil learn independently. The pupil has 'start' and 'finished' boxes with individual learning activities in plastic zip bags which allows them to organise their learning and know what 'finished' looks like.
>
> After the independent learning activities are completed, I give lots of praise and reward tokens are used to help the pupil understand delayed gratification and what it's like to work towards a goal. When the reward chart is filled with tokens the pupil gets a pre-chosen reward. We give the pupil a choice of two or three things for their reward so they are not overloaded with decisions. The sorts of things that neurotypical children find rewarding may not appeal to a child with ASD, so it's important to find out from the pupil what will motivate them. This pupil loves having ten minutes to look at the fish tank and twiddle a pipe cleaner.

Reflect

1. Look at the examples of how to make your classroom 'communication-friendly' on page 89. Is there anything practical you can do to make the learning environment more communication-friendly for your pupils with SLCN?

2. What opportunities do you provide for pupils to learn and revise new subject-specific words? Is there anything else you could do to support this further?

3. What experience do you have of children with ASD? If you have experience of more than one child, consider in what ways they are similar and in what ways they are different.

Further resources

The Communication Trust: www.thecommunicationtrust.org.uk.

The Communication Trust is a group of organisations supporting anyone working with children and young people with SLCN. Their website provides a range of useful information and resources, including:

- *Let's Talk About It*: A booklet for trainee or newly qualified teachers explaining what they need to know about children's communication skills.

- *Communicating the Code*: A resource to enable all practitioners to support the implementation of the Special Educational Needs and Disability Code of Practice: 0–25 years.

- A range of speech, language and communication progression tools for supporting identification in early years, primary and secondary schools.

I CAN: http://www.ican.org.uk.

The children's communication charity. Their website provides advice and guidance for practitioners in early years, primary and secondary schools.

A Guide for Teachers, Autism Education Trust: http://www.autismeducationtrust.org.uk/resources/teachers%20guide.aspx.

Online information for teachers, highlighting useful strategies for supporting pupils with autism in the classroom.

National Autistic Society: http://www.autism.org.uk/professionals/teachers.aspx.

The UK's largest provider of specialist autism services shares practical tips for teachers in this section of their website.

Chapter 6
Cognition and learning

As a mainstream teacher, many of the pupils with SEN who you come across are likely to have some kind of cognitive difficulty. Children and young people with cognition and learning issues will find it hard to keep up in most, or all, of the academic areas of the curriculum. They are likely to face challenges with developing basic literacy or numeracy skills and may find listening, paying sustained attention and comprehending difficult. Many pupils will also struggle with both long- and short-term memory.

Not only will the majority of these pupils struggle academically, but their all-round development could also be delayed. A pupil with cognitive difficulties may also have problems with gross motor skills, such as throwing a ball, and fine motor skills, such as holding a pencil or cutting with scissors. Some may also have poor organisational skills. If pupils become frustrated with their learning because of these challenges, they may start to use avoidance techniques or demonstrate restless or disruptive behaviour. Pupils with cognitive difficulties are unlikely to progress as quickly as their peers, and there will be a tendency for any gaps in attainment to widen as pupils get older.

Cognition and learning difficulties include:

- MLD
- SpLD
- SLD
- PMLD

Some pupils with SLD and many pupils with PMLD will be educated within specialist provision, as their needs are often very complex. Pupils with PMLD will have significant developmental delay, will often communicate non-verbally and may have additional sensory impairments and complex health needs.

Did you know?

All pupils with PMLD require high levels of support in most aspects of their daily lives and need specialised and very personalised teaching approaches. For further information on PMLD, take a look at the PMLD network at: http://www.pmldnetwork.org.

Moderate learning difficulties (MLD)

Pupils with MLD tend to find learning in most areas of the curriculum difficult. Their attainment in core areas of the curriculum, particularly English and maths, is likely to be low when compared to the majority of their peers and they do not always make progress at the same rate as others. One of the most significant barriers to learning for many pupils with MLD is a difficulty in developing basic literacy skills. If you think about the amount of time a pupil spends, on average, applying reading or writing skills across the curriculum, it's not difficult to understand why they don't just have challenges in English lessons, but also find many other subjects difficult to access.

If a pupil experiences challenges in learning to read it could be because they have problems recognising words or don't understand what they have read, or a combination of both. As a result, they may demonstrate some of the following traits:

- an inability to link letters to sounds or blend/segment phonemes

- confusing similar letters or words

- an ability to recognise a word on one page but not on another

- using information from pictures or prior knowledge to try to make sense of text, rather than what they've read

- reading on even when what is being read doesn't make sense

- finding reading or writing activities stressful

- making errors with spelling

- having limited vocabulary

Pupils with learning difficulties may take longer than their peers to assimilate new vocabulary or concepts. They will need time to practise and reinforce (known as 'overlearning') and will often have to put twice as much effort in to produce the same amount of work. This means they can become tired and may need short breaks in between tasks.

Memory plays a large factor in learning and if a pupil has poor working memory this can result in problems with processing, retaining and recalling information or a difficulty in remembering common facts, including mathematical facts such as number bonds and times tables. A pupil with MLD may also have poor listening skills and a short attention span, meaning they will find it tricky to understand and follow instructions. They may also have difficulty understanding abstract ideas such as time.

Classroom strategies

Reading

Prioritising the development of reading skills is key because of the potential impact across the whole curriculum. Based on a relatively simple view of the reading process, there are two key components that affect someone's ability to become a fluent and successful reader; word recognition and language comprehension. Although the two are related, they each require specific kinds of teaching strategies so it is important to find out in which area a pupil is struggling. For some pupils with MLD it will be both.

To support a pupil to develop their word recognition skills:

- Encourage them to sound out regular words (those that follow common phonic or spelling patterns) and blend the phonemes – e.g. *c/a/t*.

- Encourage them to recognise letter chunks or patterns within words – e.g. *a/g/ai/n* and *t/r/ai/n*; find common endings – e.g. *-ing, -tion*; or count the number of syllables – e.g. *am/bu/lance* has 3 syllables.

- Teach irregular words (those that don't follow common phonic or spelling patterns) using letter names and as sight words that are automatically recognised – e.g. said.

- Where appropriate, ask the pupil to look at a picture or use their prior knowledge about the book/paragraph/sentence to help them decide if a word makes sense.

- Encourage the pupil to read on past an unfamiliar word or read the sentence more than once and look for clues to help them recognise the word.

 Try it!

High interest, low reading level texts

For pupils who have difficulties with reading, finding materials that will keep them interested in the reading process and enable them to see themselves as readers is crucial. Many companies offer high interest books suitable for pupils with a lower reading age that do not appear too childish. Take a look at the following examples:

- Barrington Stoke (for Key Stages 1 to 4): http://www.barringtonstoke.co.uk.

- Crown House Publishing's The College Collection (for Key Stages 2 to 3): https://www.crownhouse.co.uk/publications/the-college-collection-set-1-the-complete-set.

- HarperCollins' Read On Series (for Key Stage 3): http://www.collins.co.uk/category/Secondary/English+and+Media+Studies/Read+On.

To develop reading comprehension skills:

- Pre-prepare the pupil before they read a text by discussing the cover illustration, title, synopsis and contents page to predict what type of text it is, the genre and the theme. Introduce them to the key vocabulary they will come across in the text that they might find difficult.

- Provide the pupil with opportunities to read whole texts so they can get a better sense of the context and meaning (and because reading whole texts is often more enjoyable than just reading extracts).

- Pair the pupil up with a reading buddy so they can share the reading and discuss the text together.

- Provide opportunities for pupils to practise specific comprehension skills, such as predicting, questioning, clarifying and summarising.

Many pupils who have a low reading age do not necessarily enjoy reading because of the effort that it requires. Encourage a positive attitude to reading by exposing them to a range of materials, such as magazines, leaflets, online blogs or ebooks, and by modelling the reading process yourself. This is something parents could also be encouraged to try. As well as listening to their child read, could they read aloud to their child? This strategy will enable their child to access stories that may be beyond their current reading level but within their zone of understanding.

Writing

Being a great writer is complex as there are so many skills involved – you need to be able to generate ideas and plan your work, spell, use appropriate grammar and punctuation, make the writing interesting for the reader, check your work and so on. To support the struggling writer, it's important to have a clear understanding of which elements of the writing process they find particularly challenging:

- If the pupil struggles with generating ideas, provide some high-impact stimuli to help their creativity. This could include books, stories or poems, audio or video clips, pictures or photographs, real-life objects or role-play. Make sure the writing has a real purpose to it so pupils can see the value.

- Allow the pupil to discuss their ideas with a talk partner to help them articulate their thoughts. Receiving positive affirmation of their ideas will also help develop a reluctant writer's confidence. Later on in the writing process, encourage them to ask a peer or TA to read their work out loud or record the reading so they can play it back. This can help with spotting errors and understanding where improvements can be made.

- Encourage the pupil to record their draft plan on their own whiteboard. This way they can feel confident about recording ideas without feeling they are set in stone.

- Rather than starting with a blank sheet, scaffold the planning process for the pupil by providing a graphic organiser, such as a writing frame, mind map or flow diagram. Alternatively, they could write their ideas on sticky notes – one main idea on each note – they can then move these around as they try to organise their thoughts.

 Case study

Shenaz Ibrahim, former SENCO and humanities teacher at Bolton Muslim Girls' School, explains how she scaffolds writing support for her Year 9–11 BTEC health and social care groups:

> I introduce extended pieces of writing by using draft writing frameworks and model examples. These help learners to think prior to drafting their own assignments. The inclusion of subheadings prompts learners to write topical paragraphs. Both pre-writing and draft writing help learners to think critically and use strategies consistent with our understanding of the writing process. Once learners understand when and how to use the writing frameworks, the scaffolding is gradually removed so that, eventually, they become independent writers.

If a pupil struggles with the physical aspects of handwriting, check that they are sitting in an appropriate position. For most writers, the best posture is sat up straight with their legs at right angles and their feet on the ground. Discuss the choice of writing implement with the pupil to decide which will be best to use. Some pupils will prefer pencils to pens, or prefer pens that are thicker. Others may benefit from continuing to write on lined paper so they have a guide to the size and positioning of letters. Occasionally, having an adult scribe for them means the pupil can concentrate on thinking about their ideas rather than focusing on the technical aspects of the process. Alternatively, teach them to touch-type and provide them with regular access to a laptop or PC. There are a range of software products available that can make writing more accessible, for example:

- Clicker 7: A word processor that includes resource grids to give pupils instant access to words, pictures and sounds: www.cricksoft. com.

- Texthelp Read&Write Gold: A flexible toolbar containing support features such as a text-to-speech facility: http://www.texthelp. com/en-gb.

- Inspiration: Mind mapping software that enables pupils to draw a spider diagram then turn it into a linear essay: http://www. inspiration.com.

Spelling

Practise, practise, practise is the mantra for learning spellings! Providing pupils with a framework to use can be helpful. Try one such as Look, Say, Count, Cover, Think, Write, Check. Using this strategy pupils look carefully at the word, say it aloud, count the number of letters, cover it up, write down any strategies they can use to help them remember the spelling and then try writing it from memory three times, checking once they have finished.

Playing spelling games will make learning keywords more enjoyable. One example, dicey spellings, is outlined further on in this chapter; however, there are also a number of commercial word games available that pupils can play to practise spelling and vocabulary. Why not try:

- Scrabble, Scrabble Junior or My First Scrabble
- Bananagrams
- Boggle or Boggle Junior

While we want pupils to become accurate spellers, be careful not to get hung up on correcting every mistake when marking their written work as this can be disheartening for them. Marking should be focused on the learning objective – if this isn't related to spelling, don't worry too much about correcting this aspect of the work. You may want to point out one or two words that have been practised recently where you *expect* the pupil to be using the correct spelling, otherwise, stick to commenting on the objectives.

Working memory

Working memory refers to our ability to temporarily store and process information and is key to the process of learning. Working memory has limited space so if you try to juggle too many facts at once, you are likely to lose track fairly quickly! If one of your pupils has poor working memory, they will struggle with following instructions, learning to read through a phonic approach, mental maths, problem solving and remembering topic knowledge.

 Did you know?

Gathercole and Alloway suggest that in an average class of thirty 7-year-olds there will be a six year range in working memory capacity and three children will have the working memory capacity of a 4-year-old.[1]

---

1   Susan E. Gathercole and Tracy Packiam Alloway, *Understanding Working Memory: A Classroom Guide* (London: Harcourt Assessment, 2007), p. 7.

To support a pupil who struggles with their working memory, make sure they're not presented with too many instructions at once. Alternatively, record verbal instructions or write instructions down so the pupil can refer back to them at any point during the lesson. Encourage them to use actions to remember keywords and allow them to write down the steps when calculating mathematical problems, rather than relying on their memory.

Providing memory aids such as personal memory cards, writing aids such as word mats or mathematical aids such as multiplication grids or number lines can help. Encouraging the pupil to use mnemonics to remember sequences of information can be fun (e.g. Richard Of York Gave Battle In Vain to remember the colours of the rainbow). This also includes acronyms (e.g. PEE – point, example, explain. Often, the ruder the better for remembering!).

 Try it!

The Roman room technique (or pegging)

This is a technique used to help recall a number of items of information. Ask the pupil to visualise a place they know well, such as their bedroom. The pupil then thinks about the key features of their bedroom and 'pegs' a piece of information onto each feature. They repeatedly imagine walking through the room, recounting the information as they get to each feature. This could even be done literally at first. The idea of the technique is that unfamiliar information will be linked or pegged to familiar information, locking it into the pupil's long-term memory.

Before starting to explain a new concept, find out what pupils already know by asking them to write a list or draw a mind map of key information. Pool all the knowledge and shape your explanations around these shared ideas. Begin by filling gaps and identifying any misconceptions before building in the new learning. If pupils are finding it difficult to understand abstract concepts, try turning them into a story as pupils are more likely to attend to and remember narrative than other forms of information. If you can, include any personal anecdotes – pupils love this!

Homework help

It can be particularly challenging for pupils who find writing difficult to copy down or record homework; this usually happens near the end of the lesson and is often rushed. Instead of expecting pupils to copy from the board, use labels with printed homework instructions that they can stick directly into their planners or homework diaries, or put homework onto the network system so pupils can access it from outside school. Check the readability level of any text you provide as part of the homework task and consider how challenging it will be for the pupil to complete the homework independently. If the pupil is used to receiving support from a peer or an adult in class, they will need to be taught strategies to work independently at home.

Specific learning difficulties (SpLD)

SpLD is a term used to describe a range of difficulties including dyslexia, dyspraxia and dyscalculia. The most obvious sign that a pupil has an SpLD is that they make markedly better progress in some areas of the curriculum than others. It is very common for a pupil to have traits of more than one SpLD (e.g. dyslexia and dyscalculia). This is known as co-occurrence and happens because there are a number of traits that are shared between disorders (e.g. poor working memory). Knowing the strengths and difficulties of each individual pupil is the starting point to understanding the nature of their needs and supporting them effectively.

Dyslexia

Dyslexia is a lifelong condition that primarily affects the skills involved in accurate and fluent word reading and spelling. It is often inherited and occurs across a range of intellectual abilities. Pupils with dyslexia may have difficulty processing and remembering information they see and hear. This can affect learning, in particular the development of literacy skills, sequencing and working memory. Dyslexia occurs on a continuum, so some pupils may demonstrate mild difficulties, while others can experience more significant problems.

 Did you know?

According to the British Dyslexia Association (BDA) up to 10 per cent of the population show some signs of dyslexia.[2] In an average class, that equates to approximately three children.

A pupil with dyslexia may enjoy being read to and may have good comprehension skills but have difficulties decoding text. They may:

- Struggle with phonological awareness – e.g. identifying sounds in words, identifying syllables, rhyming, blending and segmenting letters.

- Find it hard to recognise high frequency words.

- Confuse similar letters or words, either when spoken or written, often using substitute words.

- Read letters in reverse – e.g. b and d, or p and q.

- Struggle to track or focus on words on the page.

---

2   See http://www.bdadyslexia.org.uk/about.

They may demonstrate creativity and develop excellent ideas for writing. However, the technicalities of the writing process are more of a challenge as they can often have difficulties with:

- planning, sequencing and organising thoughts and ideas

- writing letters the correct way round or mixing up upper and lower case letters

- spelling (sometimes because of a poor understanding of phonics)

- copying from the board

- handwriting (if they also have difficulties with fine motor skills)

Poor working memory can mean a pupil is unable to remember sequences, dates or times tables. They may have difficulty recalling information, such as instructions, or remembering some familiar words. They may be slow to process written and verbal information, especially complex instructions. Dealing with these challenges can sometimes result in a child with dyslexia having low confidence and poor self-esteem.

Many young children make similar mistakes to children with dyslexia, but if the traits are severe, obvious and persist over time, the child is more likely to be identified as having an SpLD.

Classroom strategies

Many of the strategies that can be tried with pupils with MLD will also be appropriate for pupils with dyslexia. In addition, you could:

- Use an alphabet arc, if the pupil is still at the stage of learning the alphabet. This is more memorable than a line and pupils will be able to visualise it more easily. Encourage the pupil to recite a few letters at a time and demonstrate where they are on the arc. The arc can be used for spelling activities and games.

- Think about presentation when giving the pupil a handout or writing on the board. For some pupils who have visual processing problems or suffer from visual stress the contrast between black ink and white paper can be too stark. Try using off-white or cream paper to reduce glare, or blue ink as an alternative. Use off-white or coloured backgrounds on computers and interactive whiteboards.

- Choose a font that is rounded and reflects cursive script, such as Arial or Comic Sans. Size 14 font is ideal. Avoid worksheets that look too busy and break blocks of text up by including clearly labelled pictures or photographs and headings (but only ones that aid pupils' understanding of the text, don't bother with fancy graphics just so it looks nice!). Where possible, use headings or bulleted lists rather than continuous prose.

- Highlight keywords or important sentences or use different colours to represent different word types (e.g. adjectives, nouns, verbs).

- Use a multi-sensory approach. Because pupils with dyslexia can have poor auditory working memory, using visual and kinaesthetic approaches as well will support access to learning.

 Try it!

Dicey spellings (as suggested by retired SENCO Ruth Newbury)

Write each word you would like the pupil to practise on a card, then ask the pupil to choose one card, look at the word and identify letter patterns, rules, etc. Put the card out of view and give the pupil a dice to throw. They must follow the instruction corresponding to the number they throw:

1. Write the word with your eyes closed.

2. Spell the word backwards.

3. Write the word in bubble letters.

4. Write the word with the hand you don't normally use.

5. Write the word in the air with your finger.

6. Write a word with a similar meaning.

It is always important to build on the pupil's strengths and interests; a child with dyslexia may be very creative or imaginative, or have good comprehension skills. Share examples of positive role models with dyslexia, such as Steve Jobs, Muhammad Ali, Pablo Picasso or previous students in your school who have demonstrated success.

Dyscalculia

Dyscalculia is a specific difficulty with numbers and the number system. It is a condition which affects the ability to develop mathematical skills and pupils with dyscalculia find it difficult to understand basic number concepts. Due to a poor working memory, many pupils with dyscalculia struggle to learn and recall number facts as well as perform longer calculations involving more than one step, particularly if they are expected to hold each step in their head. They often lack confidence even when they produce the correct answer.

A pupil with dyscalculia may also find it a challenge to:

- Understand place value.

- Estimate and compare numbers.

- Recognise number patterns, even when represented visually.

- Memorise number bonds or multiplication tables.

- Count backwards.

- Recall units of measurement.

- Tell the time and understand concepts such as yesterday and tomorrow.

- Use and understand mathematical language.

- Recall numbers. They may use strategies to compensate for this lack of recall, other than counting.

- Remember mathematical procedures or they may fail to use rules and procedures to build on known facts (they may know that 5 + 3 = 8, but not realise that, therefore, 3 + 5 = 8).

Not as much is known about dyscalculia as dyslexia but some research suggests that somewhere between 3 and 6 per cent of the population are diagnosed as 'purely' dyscalculic (i.e. they only have difficulties with maths).[3] However, dyscalculia is often diagnosed alongside other conditions such as dyslexia or dyspraxia so the overall percentage of children and young people who have this difficulty with maths is likely to be higher.

Classroom strategies

Many of the strategies already mentioned will be worth trying, particularly if the pupil has a co-occurring condition, such as dyslexia. To support the specific challenges around maths and numbers:

■ Use lots of practical resources and manipulatives (e.g. counters, bead strings, number lines, money). Place value cards and grids will help develop an understanding of the value of digits. Playing cards, dice and dominoes can be used for a whole variety of number games and will reinforce the learning of visual patterns of numbers.

■ Where possible, link maths to real-life contexts that are concrete, practical and meaningful for the pupil (e.g. paying for shopping). When introducing shapes, relate them to real objects (we all remember that a Toblerone is a triangular prism!).

■ Teach a variety of methods for calculation and give the pupil the opportunity to decide which method is most suitable for them. Minimise the number of facts the pupil needs to know by heart and allow the pupil to make jottings to support mental calculations if they struggle with memory.

■ When developing word problems, use clear, unambiguous language and keep redundant information to a minimum. Encourage the

---

3   See, for example, Varda Gross-Tsur, Orly Manor and Ruth S. Shalev, Developmental Dyscalculia: Prevalence and Demographic Features, *Developmental Medicine and Child Neurology* (1996), 38: 25–33.

pupil to develop their own word problems to correspond to a given calculation.

- Remember that maths has a language of its own so learning new mathematical vocabulary can be a challenge. Provide the pupil with visual support for vocabulary, such as a maths words and phrases list. Where possible, include mathematical symbols alongside the words. Teaching an older pupil the root meanings of some maths words can support their understanding (e.g. tri = 3).

 Try it!

Maths snap

For reinforcement of language associated with the four main operations, try this group game.

Ask the group to think of as many alternative words and symbols for addition, subtraction, multiplication and division as they can. Write each one on a separate card. Pupils can use the cards to play snap in pairs, matching the words/symbols for each operation.

Dyspraxia

Pupils with dyspraxia have difficulties predominantly with the coordination of fine motor skills (small muscle movements) and gross motor skills (large muscle movements). It is a developmental disorder and although the exact causes are not yet known, it is thought to be the result of a disruption in the way messages from the brain are transmitted to the body. This affects a person's ability to perform movements in a smooth, coordinated way and can also affect their perception and thoughts.

Signs of dyspraxia in young children often include delays in achieving motor milestones (e.g. crawling or walking), dropping things and difficulties with balance and using knives and forks. At a later stage, they may also experience issues with the following:

- Controlling writing or drawing materials and tools. Their handwriting is often illegible and they are unable to write with speed or fluency.

- Organising equipment and managing their time.

- Skills such as jumping, skipping, riding a bike, throwing and catching.

- Getting dressed (getting ready for PE can be a real challenge!).

- Direction and location – e.g. confusion between left and right, up and down, north and south.

- Following instructions and staying on task.

- Managing their emotions (a pupil with dyspraxia may experience frequent bouts of anger or distress that they can't control).

Pupils with dyspraxia may also have difficulties with reading and spelling. Limited concentration, poor listening skills and literal understanding of language may have an effect on progress in reading and spelling. A pupil may read well, but not understand some of the concepts in the language.

 Did you know?

Dyspraxia is sometimes known as developmental coordination disorder (DCD). The Dyspraxia Foundation suggests that while DCD is often regarded as an umbrella term to cover motor coordination difficulties, dyspraxia refers to the additional problems with planning, organising and carrying out movements in the right order, that people with the condition experience.

Classroom strategies

In addition to supporting any learning challenges by trying some of the ideas given earlier in this chapter, focus on strategies that will help the pupil to develop their motor and organisational skills:

- Check that the pupil can safely move around your classroom (in a busy classroom there can be a number of things pupils can potentially bump into or trip over).

- Give the pupil lots of opportunities to practise handwriting. Provide different tactile experiences of writing; in trays filled with sand or shaving foam, in the air, on another pupil's back. Write large by drawing large letters on a whiteboard, using chalk to draw on the ground outdoors or painting letters on large pieces of paper taped to the wall.

- If the pupil has an awkward pencil grip, provide triangular pencil grips or a writing slope. If they have difficulty holding the paper, tape it to the table or place a non-slip mat underneath. Pupils often have difficulty finding where to make contact with the paper and making the required letter shape to the precise size and length. The more often they lift the pen from the paper to make the next letter, the harder this can be so teach the pupil to write in cursive script.

- Provide fun activities for pupils to practise gross motor skills using balance or wobble boards. Practise hand to hand throwing using bean bags or water-filled balloons.

- Help with personal organisation by providing timetables, lists of items needed for various activities or classes, diaries or file dividers. Suggest that the pupil carries a schoolbag with separate sections to aid organisation of books and other resources needed for different lessons. Adele, a Year 7 pupil who has dyspraxia, notes that one of the best pieces of advice she was given by her teacher when she moved to secondary school was to use a clear pencil case so she could see everything in it and easily get out only the things she needed to use in that lesson.

Case study

Andrew Crossley, acting head of school for Highgate and Carrfield Primary Academies in Rotherham, explains how he establishes an SpLD-friendly classroom:

> I provide a variety of cues to help pupils' processing skills. Information is presented clearly, with important words and phrases available to pupils on working walls and in vocabulary word banks. Care is taken that, wherever a pupil sits, they are able to access the support materials easily (for example, they don't have to turn to see the board or my face as I teach).
>
> I give instructions in small chunks then pupils are asked to paraphrase them back to the adults in the room or to a partner, checking their understanding. My modelling is clear, with information presented verbally and visually. Lessons are carefully sequenced with regular questioning to assess where pupils are in their learning. Pupils are given thinking time and allowed to jot responses to help structure more complex answers. Longer tasks are broken into smaller, manageable chunks with clear success criteria to enable pupils to process the learning in parts.
>
> The use of collaborative learning frameworks, such as Kagan's Rally Coach, enables pupils to articulate their learning to others and be assisted by a peer coach. Rally Coach involves pupils working in pairs: one solves a problem while the other coaches. Partners then swap roles for the next challenge.
>
> Establishing an SpLD-friendly classroom by using these techniques to support *all* pupils, enables those with SpLD to learn as effectively as their peers, without making them feel different or singled out.

Reflect

1. Which pupils have particular difficulties with reading as a result of their learning difficulties? What strategies do you routinely use to support them to access written materials? Why do these strategies work?

2. Do any of your pupils find it a challenge to access and/or complete their homework because of their learning difficulties? Try talking to them and discussing what else could help them to be more successful.

3. Have another look at the case study from Andrew Crossley. Can you identify two or three actions you could put in place to make your classroom more SpLD-friendly?

 Further resources

Moderate Learning Difficulties: http://www.sendgateway.org.uk/resources.moderate-learning-difficulties-mld.html.

An online resource module (taken from the Department for Education's Advanced Training Materials for Autism; Dyslexia; Speech, Language and Communication; Emotional, Social and Behavioural Difficulties; Moderate Learning Difficulties) that gives insights into the complexities of identifying and working with pupils with MLD. Includes classification and terminology of MLD, social aspects of MLD and whole school approaches to supporting pupils with MLD.

The Dyslexia-SpLD Trust: http://www.thedyslexia-spldtrust.org.uk.

A national organisation that provides support and guidance to teachers and parents of children and young people with SpLD.

The British Dyslexia Association: http://www.bdadyslexia.org.uk/educator.

This national association provides guidance for educators on both dyslexia and dyscalculia.

Dyspraxia Foundation: http://www.dyspraxiafoundation.org.uk/about-dyspraxia/.

A national charity aiming to increase understanding of dyspraxia, particularly among professionals in health and education.

Teachers' Pocketbooks: https://www.teacherspocketbooks.co.uk.

A series of easy-to-access professional development books which includes:

Dyslexia Pocketbook, Julie Bennett

Dyscalculia Pocketbook, Judy Hornigold

Dyspraxia/DCD Pocketbook, Afroza Talukdar

Chapter 7

Social, emotional and mental health difficulties

Do you teach a child who really pushes your buttons by frequently testing the boundaries? Do they often become frustrated, angry, upset, aggressive or withdrawn? Why do you think they are like this? There are of course numerous reasons why pupils display challenging behaviour and this behaviour does not necessarily mean they have SEN. It is important to look beyond the behaviour to identify its underlying cause. Is the pupil seeking attention? Are they having problems at home? Are they stuck with their learning? Or are they just bored?

Very few children misbehave simply in order to annoy their teacher (even though it can sometimes feel that way!). Only where the behaviour is as a result of an underlying difficulty would this be regarded as a special need. Some pupils may behave inappropriately because they have unmet needs. This could be due to cognitive difficulties or communication problems. Alternatively, it could be due to a range of SEMH problems.

Children and young people can experience a wide range of social and emotional challenges that manifest themselves in different ways, for example they may become:

- withdrawn

- passive

- socially isolated

- disruptive

- aggressive

- hyperactive

Many children and young people will demonstrate some of the above behaviours at particular points in their life, for example when they are under exam pressure, during the onset of adolescence or at times of transition, such as moving to a new school. However, if these behaviours are severe, persistent and long term they could well be the result of a SEMH difficulty. There are many examples of SEMH difficulties, for example anxiety, depression, eating disorders, AD or ADHD. Pupils with SEMH issues may struggle to cope with school routines or even resist going to school in the first place. They can have difficulties making and sustaining relationships or concentrating on their work. They may be the target of bullying, or engage in bullying-type behaviours themselves. Their general state of well-being is often poorer than their peers and even if a pupil does not have additional cognitive difficulties, their SEMH challenges will often cause a barrier to their learning.

 Did you know?

Emotional health can have a far-reaching influence on pupils' attainment and progress. A report from Public Health England in 2014 cites the fact that Ofsted had identified a strong link between schools that paid close attention to well-being and those that were graded outstanding for overall effectiveness.[1]

Mental health

When we talk about mental health it is a way of describing how we feel and how we cope with our emotions. The term is often interpreted in a negative manner to refer to mental health 'problems'. However, it is important to recognise that 'mental health' can be negative or positive: just like physical health, a person can have good mental health or poor mental health. Just as our physical health can be affected by various environmental or personal factors, so can our mental health. There

---

1 Public Health England, *The Link Between Pupil Health and Wellbeing and Attainment: A Briefing for Head Teachers, Governors and Staff in Education Settings* (London: Public Health England, 2014). Available at: https://www.gov.uk/government/uploads/system/uploads/attachment_data/file/370686/HT_briefing_layoutvFINALvii.pdf.

are certain risk factors that make some children and young people more likely to experience mental health challenges than others. These include:

- Having a parent with mental health or substance abuse problems.

- Suffering a long-term physical illness.

- Being severely bullied or physically or sexually abused.

- Experiencing family problems such as divorce.

- Suffering trauma or bereavement.

- Engaging in substance abuse.

- Living in poverty or being homeless.

- Having long-standing educational difficulties.

- Having unachievable or unsustainable expectations placed on them by themselves or others.

Some pupils experience worries, anxieties and difficult feelings to an extent that seriously interferes with their everyday life (e.g. being unable to go to school, sleep or socialise). If this is happening, and these feelings are becoming persistent, then the child is likely to require additional support.

Did you know?

According to the Department for Education, 10 per cent of children and young people are now diagnosed with a mental health disorder.[2] An additional 15 per cent are at an increased risk of developing a mental health disorder or have less severe emotional problems that still affect their development and learning.

---

2   Department for Education, *Mental Health and Behaviour in Schools: Departmental Advice for School Staff* (March 2016). Ref: DFE-00435-2014. Available at: https://www.gov.uk/government/uploads/system/uploads/attachment_data/file/508847/Mental_Health_and_Behaviour_-_advice_for_Schools_160316.pdf.

The extent, nature and impact of mental health problems experienced by children and young people today is alarming. Half of lifetime mental illness starts by the age of 14 and suicide is now one of the three most common causes of death in youth. Social media and cyber bullying are increasingly cited as part of the cause of the rise in emotional disorders. Some of the most common mental health disorders include:

- Depression (often includes overwhelming sadness, hopelessness, helplessness and lack of self-worth).

- Self-harm (often a coping mechanism to help manage intense emotions).

- Eating disorders (examples include anorexia nervosa and bulimia nervosa).

Although teachers should never diagnose a mental health difficulty, some of the signs to look out for, which may raise concern, include the pupil:

- Becoming worried, anxious, nervous or frustrated.

- Becoming over-sensitive to any criticism and being unable to handle teasing or personal remarks.

- Becoming very passive and lacking interest in work or social activities.

- Having poor concentration and not appearing to listen.

- Exhibiting obsessive behaviour or an all-absorbing interest in a topic.

- Becoming noisy, demanding and verbally or physically aggressive.

- Using unacceptable language.

- Finding it difficult to work with others.

- Becoming tired easily but not sleeping well.

- Giving up easily when they face challenges in life.

- Lying to others, cheating or blaming others for their own behaviour.

The nature of a pupil's difficulties will be very individual to them and may change significantly on a regular basis: a pupil may be very withdrawn and then become aggressive within a moment. Pupils may be unable to form close relationships and make friends, particularly if they feel uncomfortable in social situations. A significant proportion of pupils with mental health problems are subjected to bullying and will try to avoid coming to school for that reason. They may lack confidence or have low self-esteem. Callum, a Year 9 student who has been diagnosed with depression, says:

> One of the hardest things is I don't have any confidence to do anything. I hate it if I have to say something in a lesson because I think people will be staring at me and will laugh if I say something wrong. My teachers know this now though and they ask me quietly if I want to join in rather than calling my name out in front of the whole class.

 Try it!

Masked learning (suggested by Amjad Ali)

If pupils lack confidence or have low self-esteem, they may be reluctant to stand up and talk in front of the class. Amjad Ali, assistant head teacher at Cheney School in Oxford, suggests making some masks for them to wear to get into role. Choose characters that relate to the learning topic. Try historical characters or TV personalities (how about Alan Sugar, *The Apprentice* style?). Pupils can either speak as themselves or as their mask persona. The technique can also be used when pupils are giving peer feedback.

Take a look at https://www.trythisteaching.com/ or follow @ASTsupportAAli for further information and for other useful ideas to try in the classroom.

Whole school strategies

Developing positive mental health starts at whole school level. If you work in a school where the leaders promote emotional health and well-being in everyone and encourage all staff, pupils and parents to see mental health as everyone's business, then you're off to a good start. Whole school approaches develop a culture in which talking about emotions and mental health is the norm and where there are clear strategies for supporting any pupils who experience difficulties. Mental health and emotional well-being should be thread throughout the school curriculum to help create an open and positive atmosphere so that pupils are able to understand and talk about any issues they are experiencing.

As part of teaching pupils to be effective learners, and to develop positive emotional well-being, schools need to encourage them to become resilient. Resilience requires children and young people to have positive self-esteem and confidence, to believe in their own ability to deal with change and to have strategies for problem solving. We can support pupils to develop their resilience and emotional well-being from an early age by incorporating key knowledge and skills across the curriculum (e.g. communication skills, problem solving, understanding emotions, being an independent learner, managing failure and seeking help).

Classroom strategies

Mental health can be a really tricky subject. You may be overwhelmed by a sense of responsibility and worried about doing or saying the wrong thing. As a class teacher, you don't have to be an expert on mental health but you do need to create the right environment so pupils feel they can discuss any issues they may have, and you can contribute to reducing the stigma around mental health.

Communication

The most important thing to do is listen. Don't be afraid to ask a pupil how they are. You won't always understand what's going on or why they feel the way they do, but lending an ear can make a real difference. Make sure the pupil knows you are willing to listen to them and that your door is open for them to come and talk to you. Issues of stigma can mean that young people (and their parents) do not always want to share information about mental health problems. A survey carried out by the charity YoungMinds in 2014 revealed that around half of students in secondary school said they wouldn't talk to anyone if they became stressed.[3] Encourage your pupils to build up the confidence to talk. Pupils may not want to speak to adults about any problems they are facing, but they may be more inclined to speak to peers so try setting up buddy groups or friendship pairs to facilitate this more easily.

 Try it!

Worry box

The idea of the worry box is to allow pupils to put their worries in a safe place and move on with their day. Make one by decorating a shoe or tissue box. Once your box is complete, anyone can anonymously write or draw their worries on pieces of paper and drop them inside the box. They can choose to talk about their worries or not as they are in control.

If a child discloses that they have mental health issues it is important that you do not share information unless you have their permission and have explicitly told them that you will do so, with whom and in what format. However, for safeguarding reasons, if a pupil is at risk there are times when you are required to share information, even if they have asked you not to. Familiarise yourself with your school's procedures and policy with regard to safeguarding and if you're not sure, ask your designated senior person (DSP).

---

3 Tamsin Fidgeon, Survey Reveals Teenagers Facing Constant Onslaught of Stress, *youngminds.org*, 1 December 2014. Available at: http://www.youngminds.org.uk/news/blog/2347_survey_reveals_teenagers_facing_constant_onslaught_of_stress.

If you suspect a child has mental health difficulties that are not known to the school, you should communicate your concerns (within the bounds of confidentiality) to the relevant staff. This may be a school counsellor, school nurse, SENCO, head of pastoral care or, where relevent, DSP. To reiterate an earlier point, it is important that teachers do not take it upon themselves to try to diagnose disorders; a diagnosis should only be reached by qualified mental health professionals.

Managing inappropriate behaviour

Some pupils with SEMH difficulties such as ADHD, anxiety, depression or AD can find it difficult to manage their behaviour and will often benefit from a safe, calm and structured classroom environment (they may not be getting this at home). You might even want to create a safe place where the pupil can calm down. This might be in a corner of your classroom or elsewhere, such as a time-out room. Clear routines and procedures that pupils are regularly reminded of will help. Provide visual and verbal reminders about behaviour expectations, rules, routines and responsibilities. For example:

- When you are agreeing rules with the pupil, stick to a small number (e.g. four or five) that can be applied consistently rather than having lots that could become unmanageable.

- Be explicit about the behaviour you expect to see and model this, or point out when the behaviour is being modelled by others in the class. Remind the pupil of the rule rather than reprimanding them when they don't follow it – e.g. 'Our rule is to put our hand up if we want to ask a question' rather than 'Don't shout out if you want to ask a question!'

- Reward the pupil for demonstrating behaviours you want to see by using descriptive praise – this involves being explicit about why the praise has been given – e.g. 'I'm really pleased with the way you're sitting on your chair.' Some pupils can feel uncomfortable about praise being given to them publicly so discuss their preferences first. You could give them a discreet signal instead, such as a thumbs-up or tap on the shoulder.

- Provide the pupil with a choice when they are demonstrating inappropriate behaviour – e.g. if the pupil is refusing to sit down, say 'You can either sit back in your chair and work with the rest of your group or you can sit at the table next to my desk on your own. Which one is it going to be?' Remind them of the consequences of the choices available and make sure you follow through with them if necessary.

- Avoid confrontational situations where you or the pupil has to back down. Maintain eye contact with the pupil and use their name. Sound confident and in control, rather than using a loud voice and threatening gestures. Talk to the pupil in terms of their choices and the consequences of the choices, and give them 'take up' time – e.g. 'Joe, put your mobile phone in your bag or on my desk. If you choose not to it will be confiscated.' Then walk away and wait.

Whichever strategies you try, be fair and be consistent. Get the parents on board so they use the same rules and strategies at home. Where possible, be proactive and be aware of anything that triggers unacceptable behaviour so you can intervene or distract the pupil before the problem occurs. If the pupil displays inappropriate behaviour, talk to them and try to find out why they behave as they do. It is important to convey to the pupil that, while you disapprove of their behaviour, you care about them as an individual.

Try it!

ABC analysis

This involves observing and recording a pupil's behaviour over time in order to try to identify why it's happening and make positive changes. ABC refers to:

Antecedent – the events or circumstances that led up to the behaviour.

Behaviour – the behaviour in detail (what the pupil did).

Consequences – the actions or responses of the pupil or others around them as a result of the behaviour.

Record the antecedents, behaviours and consequences on a chart each time they occur. Breaking down the behaviour in this way can help you and the pupil to identify any patterns and consider the following:

- Are there similar events that lead up to inappropriate behaviour?

- Are the behaviours ones the pupil commonly displays or are they often different?

- Are the consequences driving the behaviour in the first place?

- What changes can we make so that the pupil demonstrates more positive behaviours?

Helping pupils to understand why they react in certain ways and how they can control their reactions is key to them being able to manage their own behaviour. Providing structured support with social skills through a nurture group or circle of friends approach can help, although there are a number of strategies you can use day-to-day:

- Ensure the pupil knows it's ok to have and to express different emotions. Agree with the pupil what appropriate and inappropriate ways of expressing anger, or any other emotion they may feel, look like.

■ Teach the pupil appropriate ways of telling someone when they are feeling angry or upset. Provide them with starter phrases, such as 'I am feeling unhappy because …' or 'I don't like the way that you …' Use symbols, such as faces, to show different emotions. Teach the pupil what each one means and ask them to point out the symbol which reflects how they feel.

■ Teach the pupil to understand what happens to their body when they get angry – e.g. their heart rate increases and their muscles tense up. Show them exercises or techniques they can do to relax and lower their heart rate, such as deep breathing or clenching and relaxing their fists.

 Case study

Maria Constantinou, deputy head and inclusion leader at St Mary's Church of England Primary School in Barnet, explains how she supports pupils with mental health difficulties:

> One of the most important strategies we use to support pupils with mental health difficulties is to build positive relationships by getting to know them and involving them in making decisions. At the start of the year, we use the creation of the Pupil Passport as a means of capturing all the important information a pupil wants to offer. This is the first step in creating a connection with them. Members of staff sit down with the pupil and, by taking the time to listen, we become equipped with personally and educationally crucial information that become key ingredients in ensuring the delivery of high-quality teaching.
>
> During the discussion with one particular pupil, he showed a deep understanding of his difficulties and was able to express ideas about how to manage his behaviour in school. It was important to him that he maintained his relationships with his friends, had fun and controlled his temper, even though he finds this hard when people annoy him and when things don't go his way. Under the 'what I like most' section of his passport were the words 'tarantulas' and 'dinosaurs' – a really useful nugget of information. This

provided a gateway for members of staff who work with him to engage him in learning tasks and discussion – it was interesting how many times spiders and dinosaurs featured in conversations! Giving him a voice and an opportunity to be part of the decision making process about his provision has been invaluable.

If pupils have complex SEMH issues, they are likely to require more expert help from other professionals such as counsellors or the child and adolescent mental health services (CAMHS). If you think one of your pupils would benefit from this sort of support, talk to your SENCO.

Attention deficit hyperactivity disorder (ADHD)

ADHD is a biological brain-based condition in which people find it very difficult to focus their attention or control their behaviour. Pupils with ADHD usually cannot concentrate for long, are easily distracted and often do or say things without thinking. There are three main areas of difficulty:

1. Hyperactivity – the pupil is often restless, can't sit still, talks a lot, fidgets, runs or climbs excessively.

2. Inattentiveness – the pupil lacks self-control, acts without thinking, interrupts or blurts out inappropriate comments, talks back, loses temper, can appear aggressive.

3. Impulsiveness – the pupil is disorganised, has difficulty keeping on task, appears easily bored, is forgetful, loses things, makes careless mistakes, doesn't seem to listen.

Of course, all children can behave impulsively and find it hard to concentrate sometimes, but with ADHD this behaviour is persistent and occurs wherever the child is, not just in one place such as at school or at home. There are different types of ADHD: inattentive, over-focused and classic, each one being based on the types of behaviour the child most commonly displays.

Did you know?

ADD is an additional need which is similar to ADHD. Pupils have difficulties with concentration and may appear to be daydreaming, but they don't necessarily display hyperactive, disruptive behaviours.

Symptoms of ADHD usually start when a child is a toddler, and nearly always before they reach the age of 6 or 7. Children can have ADHD in varying degrees of severity, and sometimes it is found together with other conditions such as dyslexia or dyspraxia. Estimates vary but recent studies have shown that about 5 per cent of the population has some form of ADHD, with 1 to 2 per cent having significant levels of ADHD. It is more commonly diagnosed in boys than girls.[4] Until recently, it was believed that children outgrew ADHD in adolescence, because sometimes hyperactivity seems to lessen in teen years. It is now known, however, that many symptoms continue into adulthood. There has been a lot of research into the causes of ADHD in recent years and, although the exact cause is still unknown, it is thought that it could be due to an imbalance of chemicals in the brain. Certain drug therapies are used to re-balance these chemicals and can help the child to focus their attention. However, their use is controversial as some people say it simply masks the behaviours.

Pupils with ADHD are often impulsive, quick tempered, demanding, impatient and unpredictable. They can experience difficulties with the following:

- focusing on conversations or instructions and staying on task

- remembering to bring the right equipment and resources to school

- organising their work and prioritising

- adjusting to frequent changes of activity

---

4   See the prevalence summary in ADDISS, *ADHD: Paying Enough Attention? A Research Report Investigating ADHD in the UK* (2004). Available at: http://www.addiss.co.uk/payingenoughattention.pdf.

- considering the consequences of their actions on others or seeing others' perspectives

- coordinating actions and sitting still

- waiting and turn-taking

- developing verbal expression – they may have problems sequencing words or may stutter or mumble

- developing a sense of danger

ADHD affects a pupil's cognitive capacity. They may have poor working memory and it may require more effort for them to think and process or recall information. It is believed that around half of all people with ADHD suffer from sleep disturbance, so in the afternoon it can be particularly challenging for a pupil with ADHD to continue concentrating in class!

Classroom strategies

Many of the strategies around communication and managing behaviour mentioned earlier in this chapter will support a pupil with ADHD. They will benefit from a structured environment, where there is a calm yet positive atmosphere and rules and expectations are clear and consistent.

- Consider the most appropriate place to seat the pupil so they are near to you and to good role models but not seated too close to potential distractions such as windows or heaters.

- Have a clear routine at the start of the lesson, where the pupil is expected to immediately begin a task as soon as they enter the classroom – e.g. write the date and title in their book or answer a question on the board.

- Keep instructions clear and simple. Use the pupil's name to get their attention before you start giving them instructions and encourage the pupil to maintain eye contact with you. Ask the pupil to repeat the instructions back to you to check understanding, or show you what they should be doing.

■ Give clear expectations of the amount of work you expect by a given time – e.g. 'I expect you to have at least drafted the opening paragraph by half past ten.' Provide regular time updates or give the pupil a clock/stopwatch/timer to monitor their own tasks.

■ Provide support with routines and organisation. Use timetables, organisers, planners, timers and strategies for remembering homework.

■ If the pupil starts to lose focus during class or group discussions, get them to tune back in to the lesson by directing a question at them. During longer tasks, build in a movement break for the pupil. This might mean allowing the pupil to go to an agreed quiet area of the classroom or go on a short errand.

Try it!

Using a fidget

Constantly trying to get a pupil with ADHD to stop fidgeting can cause a great deal of frustration and anxiety for the child (because they simply can't do it!). This can lead to other, more undesirable behaviours. Allowing the pupil to fiddle with an agreed object, sometimes known as a fidget, can be a good way to redirect the child's need to move, and allow them to be more focused. Try a piece of sticky tack or play dough, a squeeze ball, worry stone, pipe cleaner or something similar that the pupil can manipulate but that won't distract others!

It is important to build on the pupil's strengths and interests – talk to them to find out what motivates them and what they are good at – a person with ADHD may be very creative, imaginative and enthusiastic. Discuss examples of famous people who have ADD (e.g. Richard Branson, Michael Phelps) and encourage the pupil to see them as positive role models.

Case study

Mandy Nicholls, a Year 4 teacher at Four Dwellings Primary Academy, describes some of the strategies she uses to support two of her pupils with ADHD:

> I have two boys in my class who have ADHD. We use a visual timetable, which I run through with them each morning and explain any changes to routine. The boys check the timetable regularly to see how the day is progressing, maybe to see how much longer to break or lunchtime. When giving instructions I try to keep them simple and then ask the boys to repeat them back to me. I give a lot of praise, always explaining why they have received it – e.g. 'Well done for concentrating on that piece of writing for such a long time. I can see you have tried really hard.' They are often the children who are given the jobs around the classroom – collecting in the books or tidying up the pencil pots – as this gives them permission to be moving and using up some excess energy.

 Reflect

1. Over the last few years, there has been a significant increase in the number of children and young people identified as having mental health difficulties. What factors increase the likelihood of some of your pupils suffering from mental health difficulties?

2. Re-read the section on page 130 about whole school strategies to support good mental health. Does this sound like your school? If so, what impact are these strategies having on pupils' well-being? If not, could you have a quiet word with a senior member of staff and ask them if there's anything you can do to help develop more awareness?

3. Take a look around your classroom. Is there anything that could be a distraction for pupils with attention difficulties? How could you make changes?

 **Further resources**

Promoting Children and Young People's Emotional Health and Wellbeing: A Whole School and College Approach: https://www.gov.uk/government/publications/promoting-children-and-young-peoples-emotional-health-and-wellbeing.

Guidance for leaders on the principles behind promoting emotional health and well-being.

YoungMinds: http://www.youngminds.org.uk.

The website of the UK's leading charity committed to improving the emotional well-being and mental health of children and young people. The website includes information for professionals.

You Know the Fair Rule: Strategies for Positive and Effective Behaviour Management and Discipline in Schools, **Bill Rogers**

A practical and realistic guide to classroom behaviour management and dealing with disruptive pupils.

Attention Deficit Disorder Information and Support Service: www.addiss.co.uk.

A national organisation providing information, training and support for parents and professionals in the fields of ADHD and related difficulties.

Chapter 8

Sensory and/or physical needs

Some pupils will need special educational provision because they find it difficult to access the educational facilities usually provided within school. They will require adaptations to the curriculum or to their physical environment. Children and young people with VI or HI may require specialist support and equipment to access their learning. Those with a MSI have a combination of visual and hearing difficulties and are likely to require significant adaptations. Some children and young people with a PD will require additional ongoing support and equipment to access all the opportunities available to their peers.

Visual impairment (VI)

There are many causes of VI, depending on which part of the visual system is damaged or not working effectively. Some children with VI may be completely blind and not able to see anything at all, while some may be able to perceive light and some will be able to see up to a certain distance. Others may have a reduced field of vision (central or peripheral), see blurred images or have difficulty perceiving depth and perspective or distinguishing colour.

Often, VIs are diagnosed in children before they reach school age as issues are often picked up through concerns over motor skill delay, such as walking or holding a spoon (sight is an important part of a child's ability to learn how objects relate to each other). However, some children are not identified until later and others can develop a sight difficulty during their school years. Take note if pupils keep blinking rapidly or rub their eyes, frown or squint at work or tilt their heads. If a pupil closes or covers one eye when looking at books or turns their head to follow the line across the page when reading this *may* also be a sign of a sight problem.

? Did you know?

Pupils with VI are likely to be entitled to extra time or modified resources for internal and external examinations. If you teach a pupil with VI, check with your SENCO what access arrangements might be applicable and make sure you support the pupil to use any appropriate modifications in the classroom as part of their everyday, normal way of working.

The challenges pupils with VI face vary significantly, depending on the degree of visual loss and the nature of their impairment. Pupils may also experience delay in other areas of their development, for example:

- Language – learning new vocabulary can be a challenge if they are unable to link a visual image with the word.

- Reading – it is common for pupils with VI to confuse letters of similar appearance, miss out words or lines when reading texts, find it difficult to read from the board and find it difficult to skim and scan.

- Handwriting – pupils can have inconsistent letter formation or uneven spacing of letters within words and can experience difficulty with keeping between the lines on lined paper.

- Mobility – if peripheral vision is affected this can cause issues when pupils are moving around.

- Visual and spatial concepts – pupils may struggle with concepts such as lighter versus darker, or telling which object is bigger.

- Numeracy – pupils can face difficulties with understanding mathematical concepts such as classifying, matching, comparing and sequencing.

Pupils can often become visually fatigued when concentrating for long periods of time or suffer from frequent headaches. They may miss facial expressions, body language or other social cues and this can have an impact on their ability to make friends and interact with others.

Classroom strategies

The type of specialised teaching strategies and resources required will differ from pupil to pupil. The first step is to find out what type of VI the pupil has and how much functional vision, if any, they have. Partially sighted pupils may still use visual media such as print or pictures to learn, while pupils with no sight will rely on their other senses. Talk to the pupil, their parents and any professionals involved in supporting the pupil and share strategies with them.

Environment

At the beginning of the year, give the pupil time and support to become familiar with the classroom layout. Make sure the pupil has safe access to all areas of the room and that it is free of clutter. If you change the layout of the room during the year, give the pupil the opportunity to get used to the rearrangement. If the pupil has some residual sight, check they can see the board or any other teaching focal point. Discuss where the most appropriate place for them to sit to access teaching resources and see their peers would be (U-shaped seating is good for this). Preferably seat them in a space where the light is appropriate (e.g. not too dim or too bright). As pupils with VI often rely heavily on their hearing, try to maintain a quiet working environment. Carpet and soft furnishings such as curtains and cushions can help to improve the acoustics in your classroom.

Classroom support

- Check pupils can hear you when you are speaking, and speak clearly with extended natural pauses. Say the pupil's name before asking them a direct question and indicate who is talking during class discussions.

- Consider how you present visual materials to pupils. Experiment with different font styles and sizes. Ask the pupil which are easiest for them to read (Arial is often a preferred font as it is simple and bold). Use non-glossy, non-reflective paper and text with the greatest possible contrast (e.g. light letters on a dark background or vice versa). Don't make reading materials too cluttered – only provide necessary information.

- Where appropriate, use enlarged text or provide auditory text access. Be aware that with an enlarged version of text the pupil will see fewer words at one time so it may take longer to read.

- Rather than providing written instructions, give them verbally or voice record them prior to the lesson using descriptive and specific language. If you are putting something on the board, dictate as you write so the pupil can follow it.

- Provide opportunities for multi-sensory and hands-on learning with real-life objects and artefacts which the pupil can handle and manipulate. If necessary, assist the pupil to use resources effectively or give individual demonstrations for tasks such as cutting out or letter formation. The pupil may need the opportunity to look at and discuss any resources which will be used before the start of the lesson.

 Try it!

Reading markers

When reading, encourage a pupil who has some residual sight to use tactile markers to help them locate where they are in the book. Reading rulers, paper clips or even sticky tack can be effective.

Your school should have access to a Qualified Teacher of the Visually Impaired, a specialist who can provide guidance on teaching methods. They can support provision of additional resources and equipment such as large print, Braille, tactile maps, portable video magnifiers or computer technology, as well as offer advice on presenting and modifying learning materials and arrangements for assessments and examinations. Talk to your SENCO if you think the pupil may benefit from further specialist support.

 Case study

Matt Smith, a resistant materials teacher at Great Marlow School in Buckinghamshire, uses the following strategies when supporting pupils with VI:

> I ask the pupils to sit where they can view the board and make sure I avoid standing in front of light sources, such as windows. Printed resources are modified in a larger font size and sometimes coloured paper is used, depending on the requirements of the individual pupil. I check that any visual images are clear and high-quality.

> When writing on the board I use black pen so it stands out and I read aloud anything I'm writing. A black fine liner is used to increase the contrast for sketching and marking on pupils' work. Pupils are always provided with their own copies of books and worksheets. Wherever possible, I use real objects so they can handle any of the resources.

> Pupils will often use a laptop instead of writing and have been taught to touch-type. I allow additional time for them to complete tasks where needed. While I always encourage independence in my pupils, a teaching assistant will offer support in practical lessons for health and safety reasons.

Hearing impairment (HI)

HI is sometimes described as a 'hidden' SEN, because it is not always immediately obvious. A hearing loss may range from a very slight impairment to profound deafness and can affect either one or both ears. Loss can be temporary or permanent, depending on the cause. For example, a loss caused by a condition such as glue ear, is more likely to be temporary, but if there is damage to the mechanism of the inner ear the loss is more likely to be permanent. For a long time, it was thought that mild hearing loss has only a small impact on learning. However, recent research suggests it can have a significant effect.[1] A pupil with HI may find it challenging to hear and understand in a noisy classroom. They may be unable to pick up incidental information that is usually gained by watching and listening to others so developing language can be more difficult.

 Did you know?

A pupil with a mild hearing loss can miss up to 50 per cent of what is being said in the classroom. Imagine how difficult it is to only hear half of any conversation![2]

The difficulties faced by pupils with HI will vary depending on the degree of hearing loss, however, it is very likely that the pupil's deafness will impact on their listening skills. A pupil with HI may not hear all the words that are spoken or hear all the individual sounds in any one word. They may miss or misinterpret unstressed words in speech, for example prepositions. They may find some sounds difficult to make (e.g. 's', 'sh' and 't'). They often have poor language development and literacy skills, and

---

1   See, for example, Sue Archbold, Zheng Yen Ng, Suzanne Harrigan, et al., *Experiences of Young People with Mild to Moderate Hearing Loss: Views of Parents and Teachers* (The Ear Foundation report to NDCS, 2015). Available at: http://www.ndcs.org.uk/family_support/childhood_deafness/mild_and_moderate_hearing_loss/.
2   See Katy Morton, Children with hearing impairments struggling at school, *Nursery World*, 6 May 2015. Available at: http://www.nurseryworld.co.uk/nursery-world/news/1151244/children-with-hearing-impairments-struggling-at-school.

their vocabulary development can be limited as they don't always hear words being used in conversation around them.

In addition, a pupil may:

- miss important information, including their name being called
- ask for things to be repeated or need more time to process information and respond
- find it hard to hear when there is a great deal of background noise and struggle to locate the source of a sound
- appear to be daydreaming or fidgety
- find it difficult to join in group discussions
- struggle to regulate their own voice and either shout or whisper
- find oral work harder than written work
- become tired or frustrated because of the extra effort required
- find it difficult to develop friendships and become socially isolated

Classroom strategies

Again, the type of teaching strategies and resources that will work will differ depending on the nature of the hearing loss, so talk to the pupil and their parents and agree strategies together. Check whether the pupil is supposed to wear a hearing aid or use any other form of equipment and, if so, find out how it works. Pupils with HI are likely to lip-read to some extent, however, this takes a great deal of concentration and you will need to make allowances if they become tired towards the end of the day.

Environment

Check the acoustics in your classroom and try to minimise background noise such as heaters (or chattering!). You can improve the acoustics by having a carpet on the floor, putting rubber tips on chair legs and introducing soft furnishings such as curtains and cushions. Try not to seat the pupil near noisy equipment such as computers or projectors and check that these are turned off when not in use. If possible, arrange your desks in a circle or semi-circle so the pupil can see their peers. This is especially important if they need to lip-read. Check that there is plenty of light in the room and be aware of where you stand in the class so that the pupil can see who is speaking, can read body language and can clearly see your face if they lip-read. Try to avoid walking around the class when speaking and don't stand in front of a window as the light will be directly behind you, making it harder to see your face.

Classroom support

- Check you have the pupil's attention before speaking: otherwise they might miss the start of the conversation or instructions. Speak clearly, naturally and at your normal pace. Try not to shout or speak too slowly as this distorts lip patterns and isn't helpful for a pupil trying to lip-read! Extend natural pauses to provide the pupil with more time to process lip-reading. Repeat instructions or paraphrase what other pupils say during discussions if necessary.

- Consider using a talking stick for group discussions, so the pupil knows who is speaking. Alternatively, repeat other pupils' comments and questions, acknowledging who made the comment so the pupil can focus on the speaker.

- Provide objects and artefacts for hands-on learning or visual prompts to support communication.

- It is impossible to lip-read and take notes at the same time! Provide notes, or ask another adult or pupil to help with note taking. If pupils are working with a note taker (or interpreter), always speak directly to the pupil.

- If pupils are watching a video, use subtitles, if available, or provide transcripts. Have frequent pauses to summarise what has happened so far and reinforce any new vocabulary.

Try it!

Charades

Play charades as a way of reinforcing key learning facts as the game relies on non-verbal communication and can build on the strengths of a pupil with HI. Use it for revising book titles in English, characters in history or processes in science. Make sure the pupil catches the answer for each mime if it is called out.

HI specialists such as Qualified Teachers of the Deaf can provide help if a pupil uses alternative forms of communication, such as British Sign Language (BSL), or can provide additional resources such as hearing aids or amplified sound systems. Talk to your SENCO if you think one of your pupils may benefit from further specialist support or if you would like to know more about how you can help a pupil make the most of their aids.

Physical disability (PD)

PD is a generic term that encompasses a wide range of conditions. A pupil with PD may face challenges with hand–eye coordination, visual perception, motor movement, spatial awareness or sensory processing. Most examples can be described as long term. Many will last a lifetime, although some are age-related and are likely to change as a child gets older. Examples of PD include:

- Hereditary conditions – e.g. cystic fibrosis, haemophilia and sickle cell anaemia.

- Congenital conditions – e.g. cerebral palsy, spina bifida and hydrocephalus.

- Accidental injuries resulting in long-term or permanent disability.

- Other conditions such as asthma, epilepsy, HIV and AIDS.

Many pupils with PD will use some sort of specialist equipment. This can include specialist seating, standing frames, walkers, wheelchairs or hoists to support their movement. Some pupils may also use pillows or wedges to help them maintain their position. If pupils with physical needs also require communication support there are a range of technical aids available, such as eye-gaze systems and VOCAs.

 Did you know?

Risk assessments are required for any pupil who needs physical help to move. Anyone involved in lifting a pupil should be trained to do so.

The impact of PD on a child's learning will depend on the exact nature and degree of their difficulty and any medical conditions associated with their area of need. However, pupils may have difficulties with some or all of the following:

- Mobility and movement around the school.

- Maintaining posture – e.g. sitting upright.

- Fine motor skills – e.g. writing and cutting – and gross motor skills – e.g. running and jumping.

- Attention, concentration and memory.

- Spatial awareness or positional perception.

- Eating and drinking.

- Dressing and toileting.

- Tiredness due to the excessive energy they need to exert to perform physical tasks.

Some pupils with physical needs have no additional learning needs. However, some will also have cognitive difficulties or speech, language and communication issues. Some disabilities have related medical conditions that require regular medication or mean that the pupil is frequently absent from school. Pupils' medication may affect attention, alertness or memory and cause them to become tired, lose concentration or change their behaviour patterns. A proportion of pupils with PD will also have sensory issues.

Classroom strategies

The first thing to do when you have a new pupil with a physical difficulty is to become as well-informed as possible about their needs. Read any notes or records, and speak to the pupil, their parents and any staff or other professionals who have already been involved in supporting them. Check whether the pupil is on any medication and, if so, how this can affect their behaviour and capacity to learn. If the pupil is likely to have frequent absences from school, perhaps through illness or regular medical appointments, talk to the pupil and their parents to agree arrangements for setting homework. Make sure you are aware of any personal care requirements as some pupils may have an intimate care plan. Find out how much the pupil can do independently and when they require help.

Environment

First, it's important to ensure that a pupil with PD can access the classroom and that their immediate environment is not causing a barrier to their learning. Specialist equipment tends to take up a lot of classroom space and your classroom may need to be rearranged. If a pupil has limited mobility or uses a wheelchair or walking aid, structure your room in a way that supports them. Move any objects that will get in their way and use tables and other work surfaces that are of an appropriate height. Check they can move around the classroom easily and safely and can access their coat peg, drawer or locker. Ensure the pupil has access to appropriate seating and working positions, for example, some pupils may benefit from extra desk space or a writing slope. The hustle and bustle of a busy corridor can be a nightmare for a pupil with limited mobility so you may need to allow additional time for the pupil to move around the school. If the school has steps, doors with awkward handles or security systems, make sure they are not preventing accessibility for the pupil.

 Try it!

Checking site access

Go on a walk around the school with the pupil who has limited mobility. Identify any barriers to access together (e.g. steps, doors that are difficult to open, crowds). If your school is large, plan the best route for the pupil to get from A to B and plot it on a map for the pupil to refer back to if needed. This is particularly useful if the pupil is new to the school.

Classroom support

Due to the severity of their impairment, some children with significant physical difficulties will be highly dependent on others. It is therefore all the more important to create opportunities for them to be as independent as possible in their learning, even if they regularly have support from an adult. TAs who support physical and learning needs need to be sensitive to this and not become the total supporter, carer and best friend! No pupil should have a TA Velcroed to their side during lessons – there should always be occasions when the TA physically moves away, allowing the pupil to work independently or with a peer. Chapter 4 provides further information on the effective deployment of TAs.

Examples of effective classroom support include the following:

- Provide easy access to a variety of resources for the pupil to use so they can be as independent as possible – e.g. pens or pencils, pencil grips, writing slope, dictionaries, audio recording device, laptop.

- If the pupil's hand control is weak, provide alternative writing tools such as jumbo pencils, thick felt pens or paintbrushes held in the teeth. Specially adapted computer switches and concept keyboards can also be useful. Non-slip mats or sticky tape can also be used to hold paper or books in place.

- For a pupil who finds the physical aspects of writing really challenging, consider alternative methods of recording work – e.g. photographs, drawings, verbal responses.

- Provide opportunities throughout the day for the pupil to move around or change their position. This will help to reduce the pressure on certain parts of their body, maintain good posture and enable them to weight-bear.

- Don't forget to consider any additional arrangements needed for the pupil to access physical activities, including PE. The pupil may be able to participate fully in some activities, but may sometimes require adapted or alternative tasks that offer an equivalent degree of challenge.

Physiotherapists, occupational therapists and technical specialists can help with specific resources or specialist aids that pupils with physical impairments may need to access the curriculum. They will know what equipment and services are available and can suggest possible options.

 Case study

Eva is a Year 8 student who has cerebral palsy, a condition that affects movement, posture and coordination. Here she shares information on how teachers can support her in the classroom:

> If I have a new teacher in any of my subjects, I like it if they sit down and talk to me to ask what helps me in lessons, rather than just think they will know because they've read something on the internet! I have a Pupil Passport with lots of information about me and we can read through this together.

> As I use a wheelchair, it's easier for me to get around if the class-room isn't too jammed full of tables and chairs. It's good if I can sit quite close to the door in case I need to go out during the lesson. At lunchtime I leave the lesson a few minutes early because it gets so

crowded around school. I prefer it if the teachers let a friend leave with me so I don't have to go into the canteen on my own.

I usually use my laptop to record my work during lessons. If the teacher is showing a PowerPoint or there are some notes for the lesson, it's good if they can give me my own copy to use at the start of the lesson.

I don't want to be fussed over, that's really embarrassing. If I need help I'll ask for it. When I was in primary school I had a TA who helped me all the time. She was great but then when I started secondary school I was on my own more. I missed having her around but after a while I realised it was better for me because it made me have the confidence to try things for myself and be more independent.

The final thing to say is that teachers need to challenge me. Although I get tired easily because of my cerebral palsy, I know I can sometimes be a bit lazy with my work! My ambition is to go to university to study law: that won't happen unless my teachers push me to work as hard as I can and have the belief that I can do it. That's really important as well!

Reflect

1. Have a look around your classroom. How suitable is it for pupils with a sensory or physical impairment? Are there any changes you could make?

2. How do you ensure that pupils with a sensory or physical difficulty have full access to the curriculum in your lessons? What adaptations do you make?

3. What are some of the social barriers pupils with a sensory or physical difficulty may encounter? What else can you do to ensure pupils are fully included in your class?

Further resources

Teaching and learning guidance, Royal National Institute of Blind People (RNIB):
http://www.rnib.org.uk/services-we-offer-advice-professionals-education-professionals/
guidance-teaching-and-learning.

A series of guides including advice for early years practitioners, support for achieving independence and strategies for teaching specific subjects to children who are blind or partially sighted.

National Deaf Children's Society: www.ndcs.org.uk.

A charity dedicated to supporting children and young people who are deaf and their families. Provides free resources for schools.

The Health Conditions in School Alliance: www.medicalconditionsatschool.org.uk.

An alliance to help schools create a safe environment for children living with a medical condition. Resources available include sample healthcare plans for asthma, anaphylaxis, diabetes and epilepsy.

Scope: www.scope.org.uk.

A disability organisation offering a range of services for people affected by cerebral palsy and other disabilities, including information and support.

Final words

You will have come across a whole range of suggested approaches, strategies and ideas in this book. Try not to feel overwhelmed, take one step at a time and consider which ones are likely to have the most impact in your classroom. After reflecting on their practice, science teacher Laura Senn and geography teacher Alex Aldridge from St James' Catholic High School in Barnet, agree on their top five strategies for supporting pupils with SEN:

1. Use your Pupil Passports (or equivalent ISP) as working documents to help you gain an understanding of your pupils and refer to these when planning and during lessons.

2. Think carefully about your seating plan and where pupils with SEN will sit depending on their needs. Do they need to be near the board? Do they need to be away from distractions? Do they need support from another pupil? (Use peer support wherever possible – pupils often listen to guidance from other pupils more readily than from their teachers!)

3. Provide keywords for the lesson or topic so pupils don't need to worry about spellings, and writing frames or sentence starters to aid their organisation of written work.

4. Plan the deployment of TAs carefully. Ask them to provide targeted support, write down keywords, join in the questioning or provide prompts to help pupils participate.

5. Make sure you are consistent in your approach to behaviour management and to any type of support so pupils know exactly where they stand.

Sound advice indeed, but don't forget that no two pupils with SEN are the same and what works for one child will not necessarily work for another child. No matter what label they may have been given through a diagnosis of SEN, we must look beyond that, see the individual and get to understand their personal strengths, interests and motivation. The only way you'll really know if a strategy will be successful with a pupil is to try it out!

This book has aimed to provide an overview of your responsibilities as a teacher and outline some of the more common areas of SEN. So what if you want to find out more? Take a look at the further resources noted at the end of each chapter. These point you towards additional reading and the websites of some of the main SEND organisations. A number of these organisations also provide free (yes, free!) online professional development. Start by finding out what nasen (www.nasen.org.uk) and Disability Matters (https://www.disabilitymatters.org.uk) have to offer.

Talk to your colleagues and share ideas about how you support individuals within the classroom. Alternatively, if you work in a mainstream school, arrange a visit to your local special school or specialist setting. Staff are often willing to share their vast expertise and might also appreciate a visit to your school in return. Ask your SENCO or line manager about any other support or professional development that might be of benefit.

Teaching pupils with SEN is probably one of the most challenging aspects of our profession. It is, however, also one of the most rewarding. You can't beat that feeling of seeing the look on a child's face when they've suddenly grasped a concept or successfully completed a piece of work. It is all the more sweet when that child has put in extra effort because of the learning challenges they face. Try to be a teacher who champions the pupils with the greatest needs – it will be worth it. After all, it is you, the classroom teacher, who can make a real difference.

List of abbreviations

AAC augmentative and alternative communication

AD attachment disorder

ADD attention deficit disorder

ADHD attention deficit hyperactivity disorder

ASD autistic spectrum disorder

BSL British Sign Language

CAMHS child and adolescent mental health services

CAT cognitive abilities test

DfE Department for Education

DSP designated senior person

EEF Education Endowment Foundation

EHC education, health and care (plan)

HI hearing impairment

HQT high-quality teaching

IEP individual education plan

IOE Institute of Education

ISP individual support plan

LA local authority

MLD moderate learning difficulties

MSI multi-sensory impairment

NQT newly qualified teacher

PD physical disability

PMLD profound and multiple learning difficulties

SEMH social, emotional and mental health

SEN special educational needs

SENCO special educational needs coordinator

SEND special educational needs and disability

SLCN speech, language and communication needs

SLD severe learning difficulties

SLT senior leadership team

SpLD specific learning difficulties

TA teaching assistant

VI visual impairment

VOCA voice output communication aids

SEN glossary

Asperger syndrome – Often referred to as high-functioning autism, it leads to a difficulty in communicating, difficulty in social relationships and a lack of understanding of how people feel.

Attachment disorder (AD) – A mental and emotional condition caused by failure to form an appropriate bond with primary carers in early childhood.

Attention deficit disorder (ADD) – A difficulty resulting in the inability to maintain concentration.

Attention deficit hyperactivity disorder (ADHD) – A difficulty resulting in an inability to maintain concentration, impulsive behaviour and constant movement.

Autistic spectrum disorder (ASD) – A difficulty in understanding and using non-verbal and verbal communication.

Brittle bone disease – A condition where the bones break easily and sufferers can often have multiple fractures.

Cerebral palsy – A condition occurring before, during or after birth in which there is abnormal brain development or injury to the brain. Results in difficulties with muscle control and movement.

Chronic fatigue syndrome (also known as ME) – A condition that can occur following a viral infection; it is characterised by persistent fatigue and sometimes muscle pain.

Cognitive difficulty – Refers to difficulties caused by the way the brain retains and organises thoughts and solves problems.

Cystic fibrosis – A genetic condition affecting the lungs and digestive system.

Down's syndrome – A genetic disorder that develops when a baby is in the womb, affecting physical and cognitive development.

Dyscalculia – A difficulty in using and understanding numbers and calculation.

Dysgraphia – A specific learning difficulty that affects written expression, including handwriting and spelling.

Dyslexia – A difficulty in learning to read, write and spell, despite progress in other areas.

Dysphasia (also known as aphasia) – A language disorder affecting the ability to express and understand words.

Dyspraxia – A difficulty with coordination and motor movement.

Epilepsy – A condition that causes seizures as a result of a sudden burst of excess electrical activity in the brain.

Expressive language difficulty – A difficulty affecting the ability to speak, write or gesture.

Foetal alcohol syndrome disorder (FASD) – A condition caused by the mother drinking excessive alcohol during pregnancy, resulting in abnormal brain development.

Fragile X syndrome – A genetic condition resulting in learning difficulties.

Hearing impairment (HI) – Reduced functioning in the ability of one or both ears to detect and/or process sounds. Ranges from mild hearing loss to profound deafness.

Irlen syndrome – A specific learning difficulty that affects the way the brain processes visual information. Leads to an inability to read fluently and with ease, sensitivity to light and sensitivity to colour combinations.

Moderate learning difficulty (MLD) – Results in a general level of academic attainment significantly below peers'. Includes difficulty in acquiring basic literacy and numeracy skills and speech and language skills.

Multi-sensory impairment (MSI) – A combination of visual and hearing impairments.

Muscular dystrophy – A progressive weakness of the muscles due to a breakdown of the muscle fibre. Some conditions are life-limiting, others are milder.

Phonological impairment – A difficulty in recognising, selecting and using speech sounds in words.

Physical disability (PD) – A generic term covering challenges with hand–eye coordination, visual perception, motor movement, spatial awareness or sensory processing.

Pragmatic disorder – A difficulty in using language appropriate to a given situation.

Profound and multiple learning difficulties (PMLD) – Significant developmental delay, resulting in communication issues, additional sensory impairments and complex health needs.

Receptive language difficulty – A difficulty in understanding other people's use of language.

Severe learning difficulty (SLD) – Significant cognitive impairment.

Specific learning difficulty (SpLD) – Cognitive difficulty in one particular area. Includes dyslexia, dyscalculia and dyspraxia.

Speech, language and communication needs (SLCN) – A generic term describing difficulties in communicating with others. Includes both expressive and receptive language problems.

Tourette syndrome – A neurological condition resulting in tics, involuntary and uncontrollable sounds and movements.

Visual impairment (VI) – Reduced functioning in the ability of one or both eyes to detect and/or process images. Ranges from partial sightedness through to total blindness.

List of professionals

Clinical psychologist – A health professional who provides individual and family counselling and advice. They can advise and support on a variety of issues, including behaviour management and conditions such as autism.

Counsellor – A professional who helps people talk about their feelings. This could be because of grief, stress or to help them deal with everyday life. Many schools now employ their own in-school counsellors to support pupils and their families.

Designated senior person (DSP) – a senior member of the school's leadership team who takes lead responsibility for dealing with safeguarding issues.

Educational psychologist – A specialist who carries out assessments of learning and emotional needs and provides advice to schools and parents. They will become involved if a child is having an education, health and care (EHC) plan assessment.

Health visitor – A health professional responsible for supporting the development of pre-school children and children with disabilities. Health visitors will visit families at home when a child is born and they also offer advice to families on general child development and health issues.

Occupational therapist – A health professional who supports children who have difficulty carrying out everyday activities (e.g. dressing, walking, feeding) because of some form of physical, psychological or social delay or disability. They often provide advice and access to specialised equipment.

Paediatrician – A doctor specialising in the care of babies and children. They can assess, identify and diagnose delay, disorders or medical conditions in children, including autism.

Physiotherapist – A health professional supporting children and young people who have physical and motor developmental delay. They give advice and plan individual activity programmes for posture, coordination and movement and can also advise on specialist equipment.

Social worker – A health and care professional who safeguards and promotes the welfare of vulnerable children. They work with children and their families to help them thrive.

Specialist teacher – A teacher who provides support and guidance within their specialist area. They may be part of a local outreach service. Specialist teachers include Qualified Teachers of the Deaf and Qualified Teachers of the Visually Impaired.

Speech and language therapist – A specialist who provides support for language, communication and speech needs. They develop specialist programmes to support individual children and also provide training and advice to school staff.

References and further reading

ADDISS (2004). *ADHD: Paying Enough Attention? A Research Report Investigating ADHD in the UK*. Available at: http://www.addiss.co.uk/payingenoughattention.pdf.

Archbold, Sue, Yen Ng, Zheng, Harrigan, Suzanne, Gregory, Sue, Wakefield, Tina, Holland, Lynda and Mulla, Imran. (2015). *Experiences of Young People with Mild to Moderate Hearing Loss: Views of Parents and Teachers* (The Ear Foundation report to NDCS). Available at: http://www.ndcs.org.uk/family_support/childhood_deafness/mild_and_moderate_hearing_loss/.

Bennett, Julie (2014). *Dyslexia Pocketbook*. Alresford: Teachers' Pocketbooks.

Bentley-Davies, Caroline (2010). *How to Be an Amazing Teacher*. Carmarthen: Crown House Publishing.

Blatchford, Peter, Bassett, Paul, Brown, Penelope, Martin, Clare, Russell, Anthony and Webster, Rob (2009). *The Deployment and Impact of Support Staff Project*. Research Brief: DCSF-RB148. London: DCSF. Available at: http://maximisingtas.co.uk/assets/content/dissressum.pdf.

Bosanquet, Paula, Radford, Julie and Wester, Rob (2016). *The Teaching Assistant's Guide to Effective Interaction: How to Maximise Your Practice*. Abingdon: Routledge Education.

Budd Rowe, Mary (1987). Wait Time: Slowing Down May Be a Way of Speeding Up, *American Educator* 11 (Spring): 38–43. EJ 351 827.

Communication Trust (2013). *A Generation Adrift: The Case for Speech, Language and Communication to Take a Central Role in Schools' Policy and Practice*. London: The Communication Trust.

Csikszentmihali, Mihaly (1990). *Flow: The Psychology of Optimal Experience*. New York: Harper and Row.

Department for Education (2001). *Special Educational Needs Code of Practice*. Ref: DfES/581/2001. Available at: http://webarchive. nationalarchives.gov.uk/20130401151715/https://www.education.gov. uk/publications/eorderingdownload/dfes%200581%20200mig2228.pdf.

Department for Education (2009). Advanced Training Materials for Autism; Dyslexia; Speech, Language and Communication; Emotional, Social and Behavioural Difficulties; Moderate Learning Difficulties. Available at: http://www.advanced-training.org.uk/.

Department for Education (2012). *Teachers' Standards*. Available at: https://www.education.gov.uk/publications/eOrderingDownload/ teachers%20standards.pdf.

Department for Education (2013). *The National Curriculum in England Framework Document*. Available at: https://www.gov.uk/government/ uploads/system/uploads/attachment_data/file/210969/NC_ framework_document_-_FINAL.pdf.

Department for Education (2014). *Equality Act 2010 and Schools: Departmental Advice for School Leaders, School Staff, Governing Bodies and Local Authorities*. Ref: DFE-00296-2013. Available at: http:// www.gov.uk/government/uploads/system/uploads/attachment_data/ file/315587/Equality_Act_Advice_Final.pdf.

Department for Education (2014). *Schools: Guide to the 0 to 25 SEND Code of Practice: Advice for School Governing Bodies/Proprietors, Senior Leadership Teams, Sencos and Classroom Staff*. Ref: DFE-00558-2014. Available at: www.gov.uk/government/uploads/system/uploads/ attachment_data/file/349053/Schools_Guide_to_the_0_to_25_ SEND_Code_of_Practice.pdf.

Department for Education (2014). *Special Educational Needs and Disability Code of Practice: 0 to 25 Years*. Ref: DFE-00205-2013. Available at: https://www.gov.uk/government/publications/ send-code-of-practice-0-to-25.

Department for Education (2016). *Mental Health and Behaviour in Schools: Departmental Advice for School Staff* (March). Ref: DFE-00435-2014. Available at: https://www.gov.uk/government/uploads/ system/uploads/attachment_data/file/508847/Mental_Health_and_ Behaviour_-_advice_for_Schools_160316.pdf.

Department for Education (2016). *School Workforce in England: November 2015*. Ref: SFR 21/2016. Available at: https://www.gov.uk/government/statistics/school-workforce-in-england-november-2015.

Department for Education (2016). *Schools, Pupils and Their Characteristics: January 2016*. Ref: SFR 20/2016. Available at: https://www.gov.uk/government/statistics/schools-pupils-and-their-characteristics-january-2016.

Department for Education (2016). *Special Educational Needs in England: January 2016*. Ref: SFR 29/2016. Available at: https://www.gov.uk/government/uploads/system/uploads/attachment_data/file/539158/SFR29_2016_Main_Text.pdf.

Dweck, Carol (2006). *Mindset: The New Psychology of Success*. New York: Ballantine Books.

Education Endowment Foundation (n.d.). Teaching and Learning Toolkit. Available at: https://educationendowmentfoundation.org.uk/resources/teaching-learning-toolkit/.

Ehlers, Stephan and Gillberg, Christopher (1993). The Epidemiology of Asperger Syndrome, *Journal of Child Psychology and Psychiatry* (November), 34 (8): 1327–1350.

Fidgeon, Tamsin (2014). Survey Reveals Teenagers Facing Constant Onslaught of Stress, *youngminds.org*, 1 December. Available at: http://www.youngminds.org.uk/news/blog/2347_survey_reveals_teenagers_facing_constant_onslaught_of_stress.

Gathercole, Susan E. and Alloway, Tracy Packiam (2007). *Understanding Working Memory: A Classroom Guide*. London: Harcourt Assessment.

Griffith, Andy and Burns, Mark (2012). *Engaging Learners*. Carmarthen: Crown House Publishing.

Griffith, Andy and Burns, Mark (2014). *Teaching Backwards*. Carmarthen: Crown House Publishing.

Gross-Tsur, Varda, Manor, Orly and Shalev, Ruth S. (1996). Developmental Dyscalculia: Prevalence and Demographic Features, *Developmental Medicine and Child Neurology*, 38: 25–33.

Hattie, John (2012). *Visible Learning for Teachers: Maximising Impact on Learning*. Abingdon: Routledge.

Henderson, Anne T. and Mapp, Karen L. (2002). *A New Wave of Evidence The Impact of School, Family, and Community Connections on Student Achievement*. Austin, TX: Southwest Educational Development Laboratory and National Center for Family and Community Connections with Schools. Available at: https://www.sedl.org/connections/resources/evidence.pdf.

HMSO (1978). *Report of the Committee of Enquiry into the Education of Handicapped Children and Young People*. Available at: http://www.educationengland.org.uk/documents/warnock/warnock1978.html.

Hornigold, Judy (2015). *Dyscalculia Pocketbook*. Alresford: Teachers' Pocketbooks.

Morton, Katy (2015). Children with hearing impairments struggling at school, *Nursery World*, 6 May. Available at: http://www.nurseryworld.co.uk/nursery-world/news/1151244/children-with-hearing-impairments-struggling-at-school.

nasen (2014). *SEN Support and the Graduated Approach*. Tamworth: nasen. Available at: http://www.nasen.org.uk/resources/resources.sen-support-and-the-graduated-approach.html.

nasen (2014). Working with Outside Agencies: A Framework for Consultation – Class Teacher [video]. Available at: http://www.sendgateway.org.uk/resources.working-with-outside-agencies-a-framework-for-consultation-class-teacher.html.

nasen (2015). *Working in Partnership with Parents and Carers: A Quick Guide to Ensuring That Schools Work Closely with Parents and Carers to Meet the Needs of Children and Young People with SEND*. Tamworth: nasen. Available at: http://www.nasen.org.uk/resources/resources.working-in-partnership-with-parents-and-carers.html.

Ofsted (2010). *The Special Educational Needs and Disability Review: A Statement Is Not Enough*. Ref: 090221. Available at: https://www.gov.uk/government/uploads/system/uploads/attachment_data/file/413814/Special_education_needs_and_disability_review.pdf.

Ofsted (2015). *School Inspection Handbook*. Ref: 150066. Available at: https://www.gov.uk/government/publications/school-inspection-handbook-from-september-2015.

Peacock, Alison (2016). *Assessment for Learning without Limits*. London: Open University Press.

Public Health England (2014). *The Link Between Pupil Health and Wellbeing and Attainment: A Briefing for Head Teachers, Governors and Staff in Education Settings.* London: Public Health England. Available at: https://www.gov.uk/government/uploads/system/uploads/attachment_data/file/370686/HT_briefing_layoutvFINALvii.pdf.

Public Health England (2015). *Promoting Children and Young People's Emotional Health and Wellbeing: A Whole School and College Approach.* London: Public Health England. Available at: https://www.gov.uk/government/publications/promoting-children-and-young-peoples-emotional-health-and-wellbeing.

Rogers, Bill (2012). *You Know the Fair Rule: Strategies for Positive and Effective Behaviour Management and Discipline in Schools.* Cambridge: Pearson.

Rosenthal, Robert and Jacobson, Lenore (1966). Teachers' expectancies: Determinants of pupils' IQ gains, *Psychological Reports*, 19: 115–118. Available at: http://www.indiana.edu/~educy520/readings/rosenthal66.pdf.

Sharples, Jonathan, Webster, Rob and Blatchford, Peter (2015). *Making Best Use of Teaching Assistants: Guidance Report.* London: Education Endowment Foundation. Available at: https://educationendowmentfoundation.org.uk/uploads/pdf/TA_Guidance_Report_Interactive.pdf.

Talukdar, Afroza (2012). *Dyspraxia/DCD Pocketbook.* Alresford: Teachers' Pocketbooks.

Wragg, Edward and Brown, George (2001). *Questioning in the Secondary School.* London: RoutledgeFalmer.

Useful websites

Attention Deficit Disorder Information and Support Service: www.addiss.co.uk.

Autism Education Trust: http://www.autismeducationtrust.org.uk/.

The British Dyslexia Association: http://www.bdadyslexia.org.uk/educator.

The Communication Trust: www.thecommunicationtrust.org.uk.

The Council for Disabled Children (CDC): www.councilfordisabledchildren.org.uk.

The Dyslexia-SpLD Trust: http://www.thedyslexia-spldtrust.org.uk.

Education Endowment Foundation: https://educationendowmentfoundation.org.uk/.

The Health Conditions in School Alliance: www.medicalconditionsatschool.org.uk.

Helen Sanderson Associates: http://www.helensandersonassociates.co.uk/.

I CAN: http://www.ican.org.uk.

nasen: http://www.nasen.org.uk/.

Natalie Packer Educational Consultancy: www.nataliepacker.co.uk.

National Autistic Society: http://www.autism.org.uk/professionals/teachers.aspx.

National Deaf Children's Society: www.ndcs.org.uk.

PMLD Network: http://www.pmldnetwork.org.

Royal National Institute of Blind People (RNIB): https://www.rnib.org.uk/.

Scope: www.scope.org.uk.

The SEND Gateway: http://www.sendgateway.org.uk.

SMOG readability calculator: http://www.niace.org.uk/misc/SMOG-calculator/smogcalc.php.

YoungMinds: http://www.youngminds.org.uk.

About the author

Natalie Packer is an independent education consultant who specialises in special educational needs (SEN) and school improvement. She develops and delivers a wide range of training and support to primary, secondary and special schools, local authorities and other organisations. Natalie is an associate consultant for the National Association of Special Educational Needs (nasen) and a member of the Academies Enterprise Trust (AET) SEN team, providing support for leadership of SEN and inclusion. Natalie is a consultant for a 4–18 school in Dubai and a trustee of a recently formed multi-academy trust.

Natalie has previously worked for the National Strategies SEN team and the Department for Education, helping to implement the Achievement for All (AfA) project which was designed to improve outcomes for children and young people with SEN. Prior to this, she worked for several local authorities across the East Midlands as an adviser for SEN and school improvement. She has had primary headship experience and has also been a SENCO. Natalie is the author of *The Perfect SENCO*, an essential read for those wanting to develop their strategic SEN role effectively.

🖵 **www.nataliepacker.co.uk**

🐦 **@NataliePacker**

Don't Send Him in Tomorrow

Shining a light on the marginalised, disenfranchised and forgotten children of today's schools

Jarlath O'Brien

ISBN 978-178135253-3

In *Don't Send Him in Tomorrow*, Jarlath O'Brien shines a light on the marginalised, disenfranchised and forgotten children of today's schools. The percentage of children achieving the government's expected standard in benchmark tests is national news every year. The progress that children with learning difficulties and SEND make is never discussed, because it is not understood. That is a problem. The bone-crushing infrastructure which professionals have to negotiate is a problem. The fact that so many parents have to fight tooth and nail so that the needs of their children are met, something the rest of us would consider a basic entitlement, is a problem.

This book describes how the system can be improved if and when these marginalised children are given higher priority by the powers that be.

www.crownhouse.co.uk

The Little Book of Dyslexia

Both sides of the classroom

Joe Beech edited by Ian Gilbert

ISBN 978-178135010-2

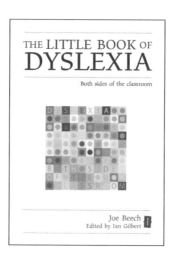

The Little Book of Dyslexia references both personal experience and current applied research and findings in order to highlight issues faced by people with dyslexia. It looks at a number of strategies and lesson ideas which can be used both inside and outside the classroom to help students with dyslexia and specific learning difficulties. It also lists various resources which can be used alongside these strategies to create a successful learning environment for those with dyslexia.

The book progresses through the various challenges that are faced at different ages and details the support needed, starting with the youngest in early years – including some of the early signs you may see with dyslexia – moving up through primary and secondary school. Finally Joe Beech discusses his experiences of higher education and university and being a student teacher.

An outstanding guide for students, teachers, special educational needs coordinators (SENCOs) and parents.

www.crownhouse.co.uk

The Little Book of the
Autism Spectrum

Dr Samantha Todd edited by Ian Gilbert

ISBN 978-178135089-8

This invaluable guide will allow anyone who lives or works with children with challenging behaviour, behaviour problems, learning difficulties or who are on the autism spectrum to see the world as they do, and develop strategies for managing and understanding autism effectively.

It peers through the 'autism lens', allowing us to understand autism and effect change in terms of the way we deal with autism as a society and in education. It delivers evidence-based support and strategies that enable us to develop young people's abilities to interact with the social world, removing much of the anxiety that often accompanies it. An essential read for anyone working with children and young people on the autism spectrum, it will also prove to be a useful parents' guide to children's mental health and emotional well-being.

www.crownhouse.co.uk

The Perfect SENCO

Natalie Packer edited by Jackie Beere

ISBN 978-178135104-8

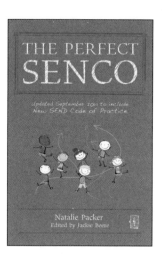

The Perfect SENCO is the fully up-to-date, essential guide to supporting children with special educational needs (SEN); an invaluable resource for all schools that are looking to update their practice in line with the new national guidelines. Revised and updated to cover the changes resulting from the new Special Educational Needs and Disability Code of Practice, this book will empower your school to embrace the national changes which came into force in September 2014, by demonstrating how to support every teacher as a teacher of children with SEN.

This updated edition is referenced against the Children and Families Act, the Special Educational Needs and Disability Code of Practice and up-to-date Ofsted guidelines. It will support SENCOs, inclusion managers and coordinators, SEN governors and senior leaders to start implementing change effectively.

www.crownhouse.co.uk